TEACHING WITH YOUR MOUTH SHUT

TEACHING
WITH YOUR
MOUTH
SHUT

DONALD L. FINKEL

FOREWORD BY
PETER ELBOW

Boynton/Cook Publishers
HEINEMANN
Portsmouth, NH

Boynton/Cook Publishers, Inc.
A subsidiary of Reed Elsevier Inc.
361 Hanover Street
Portsmouth, NH 03801–3912
www.boyntoncook.com

Offices and agents throughout the world

Library of Congress Cataloging-in-Publication Data
Finkel, Donald L., 1943–1999
    Teaching with your mouth shut / Donald L. Finkel.
        p.   cm.
    Includes bibliographical references and index.
    ISBN 0-86709-469-9
    1. Teaching.   2. Education—Experimental methods.   3. Learning, Psychology of.   I. Title.

    LB1026.F49   1999
    371.102—dc21   99–054132

Editor: Lois Bridges
Production coordinator: Elizabeth Valway
Production service: Matrix Productions
Cover design: Jenny Jensen Greenleaf
Manufacturing: Louise Richardson

Printed in the United States of America on acid-free paper
09 08 07 06 05 VP 9 10 11 12 13

This book is dedicated to
Zoe, David, Daniel, and Benjamin, my children,
and to Susan, my wife.

Contents

Foreword

PETER ELBOW

This book makes me proud to have been a colleague with Don Finkel and to have taught at The Evergreen State College (overlapping with him from 1976 to 1981). The book brings us more news about teaching and learning than most books on that topic I've read in the last decades. By "news," I don't mean "the newest, latest fashion in education"—indeed there's even something bracingly "old" to this book. What I mean is that this book gives me a fresher lens or perspective on teaching and learning than I've had in a very long time.

Teaching with Your Mouth Shut is not a "one-right-way" book that peddles a single method or technique. For example, we might expect a book with this title to take a dim view of lecturing; and it mostly does. Yet Finkel is actually eloquent about how a lecture or piece of sustained "Telling" can sometimes make "teaching with your mouth shut" more effective.

But he doesn't avoid the "one-right-way" trap by hiding behind wise generalizations and broad principles. He is openhanded in often laying out specific activities in a practical fashion, and he sometimes describes the steps he went through in a class or series of classes in such a way as to invite us to adapt, imitate, or even borrow.

Finkel avoids the low road of "one-right-way" advice and the high road of mere wisdom by creating a book that is essentially an exploration or analysis of *experience* in learning and teaching. The book functions as a kind of conversation or thinking machine to help us reconsider the most central practices in our teaching. As I was reading, I kept stopping and thinking about my own planning and teaching. The more I did that, the more powerful the book became. Early in the book, Finkel asks us to stop and do a bit of reflective writing before going further. I recommend doing so—however odd it might feel. During some periods of my reading, when I rushed to "get the ideas," I missed out on some of the insights the book later gave me when I came back to those sections less hurried.

When people talk about the importance of experience in learning, they usually imply a dichotomy between experiential learning and "mere" books, words, and concepts. Experiential learning tends to mean things like these: performing a scene, role-playing an author or character in a book, having a debate, arranging ourselves in the classroom along a line according to our "position" on some controversial issue, exploring trust and building community by closing our eyes and falling backward into the arms of classmates, going out into the woods to practice close observation or listening, or doing careful research on some aspect of the wetlands of Puget Sound for a whole quarter or even a year.

Nothing in Finkel's book argues against any of these activities, and I happen to be interested in the bodily and performative dimensions of learning. But the remarkable importance of this book comes from how Finkel demolishes the dichotomy between "mere" book-verbal-conceptual learning and "experiential learning." He zeros in on the task of designing activities to produce richly experiential learning that is not particularly bodily or performative. Finkel's whole book speaks to an idea I reflected on with some perplexity before I went to Evergreen or met him: "the profound fact about education is not that most of what students read means very little, but that occasionally, for some students, something read means a great deal" ("Nondisciplinary" 9). This book is about how to create the *experience* of abstract, verbal concepts-out-of-books.

Finkel is building on Piaget, Dewey, and James—and in particular on the powerful principle he quotes from Dewey that "no thought, no idea, can possibly be conveyed as an idea from one person to another." He hangs on to this premise with a doggedness that stems, he says, from an early moment in his teaching at the University of Washington when he was lecturing on Piaget and realized that if he actually believed what he was saying, he would have to find a way to change the way he was teaching—even with large lecture classes.

For even though he insists that learning comes only from experiences—not from words in themselves, whether heard or read—he also recognizes that words are the most convenient and efficient raw material we have in schools and colleges out of which to create experiences of genuine learning. Finkel's "conceptual workshop" is the central or paradigm example he gives for how to design situations that evoke experiences out of "merely" written words. Finkel is an ingenious architect of feasible perplexities—planned "gaps" in understanding that lead to active thinking and learning. I call him an architect because he's so interested in the structures involved in creating such experiences.

Finkel shows conceptual finesse as he looks into the guts of the thinking and learning process. He reminds me of someone who can see the innards of the internal combustion engine and tell the bits and pieces of the events inside. One small, appealing example: he shows how to design questions to help students feel a concept better by moving "from its *meaning* to its *function*."

We see here evidence of Finkel's careful Piagetian training. The book is very disciplined. I can feel how he's been reflecting on some of these techniques for three decades—refining these insights and testing these practices throughout a long career of teaching in two very opposite academic settings: large lecture courses at the University of Washington and small interdisciplinary seminars at Evergreen.

* * *

I want to call attention to the way Finkel gives us careful, clear thinking about issues that are often subtle, fuzzy, or vexed. Here are five examples that struck me.

1. *Student-centered teaching vs. teacher-centered teaching.* Finkel fights the good fight to bring students and the learning process to center stage and to push away the pervasive cultural model of the good teacher as the prominent, charismatic, performing professor. Yet I appreciate the way Finkel doesn't raise "student centered" as a banner— indeed he doesn't use either of the terms themselves. (The book is notable for the absence of jargon or fashionable terminology.) Most of all, he highlights a crucial truth that is sometimes obscured by the *teacher-centered* vs. *student-centered* terminology: teaching with your mouth shut in the ways he advocates requires lots of strong, unhidden authority, lots of planning and control of what you want to make happen, and deep understanding of the concepts that you want to get students to experience. If I were trying to find the most flat-footed title for this book, I might choose, *How to Think Through, Design, and Take Control of What You Want to Teach So That Your Students Actually Experience It.*

2. *Power vs. authority.* I sometimes get impatient when academic writers tease out fine theoretical distinctions, but I found myself grateful for the way Finkel showed the practical importance in the classroom of the difference between the teacher's power and the teacher's authority.

3. *Plato and Rousseau.* Among the numerous "Most Wanted Criminal" posters on academic walls these days, Plato and Rousseau are prominent. It's amazing how many current ills in society and education have been laid at their feet. I found Finkel's brief but carefully sympathetic readings of sections in Plato and Rousseau to be helpful and interesting—and a much needed correction.

4. *A psychoanalytic lens on teaching and learning.* This is not the central focus or theme in Finkel's book. (Piaget is central—a figure who also

turns up on some "Most Wanted" posters.) But Finkel deftly derives some useful insights from the psychoanalytic concept of *transference,* and good insights as well about the relationship between conceptual, academic learning and *character.* These insights are a good counterpoint to his Piagetian emphasis on cognition. The whole book, by the way, provides a moving counterpoint to Jane Tompkins's rhetorical use of blurted confessions and slipped decorum. Finkel's is a book of enormous decorum and control.

5. *Teacher as silent observer, as speaker, and as writer.* Given the title of the book, we shouldn't be surprised at interesting insights about silence (for instance about harnessing parables for their ellipses and non-saying; or harnessing the literal silence of a teacher in a discussion). But I'm struck with Finkel's fruitful preoccupation with a teacher's use of words and language. Finkel heightens the role of *teacher as writer:* writing out directions for conceptual workshops and writing response letters and other documents for students. And he is intriguing on the differences between the teacher as speaker and the teacher as writer. (I admired, by the way, Finkel's useful insights on helping students with their own writing.)

* * *

As I was reading this book I kept being struck by Finkel's own writing—admiring a quiet power I found difficult to describe. Let me reflect a bit on Finkel's *voice* or *presence* here.

My first impulse was to call it a nonpartisan or dispassionate voice, but as soon as I said that to myself it felt wrong. For of course the voice *is* partisan: it embodies a deep commitment to attitudes and behaviors that are largely neglected in education. Yet I think most readers will respond to a quality of quiet reflectiveness in the way he articulates a strongly felt point of view without investing it with "spin" or, in a sense, even with feeling. One seems deeply respected as a reader—as though listening to someone who is himself willing to listen.

The closest thing to feeling or "spin" is a kind of *stubbornness* I often feel in Finkel's insistence on putting things plainly, bluntly, and without embellishment. I feel an unbudging insistence on that simple premise from Dewey in all its *literalness:* "No thought, no idea, can possibly be conveyed as an idea from one person to another." Many educational reformers and radicals invoke this premise but few really hew to it as Finkel does. I also feel a stubborn literalness when he insists that his goal with "mere words" is to produce "significant change in human behavior."

It's a quiet voice, and yet I hear a resonance. Perhaps I'm influenced here by actually hearing Don's voice as I read off the page. Though I haven't seen him in many years, I have spoken with him on the phone a few times. He has a quiet, unhurried, deep voice. Yet I don't think I'm just being fooled by acoustic memory. Finkel has somehow managed to embed this voice quality *into* his words on the page. (Of course this matter of "voice in writing" is a mysterious and subjective affair—but it's one that I keep exploring; see my Introduction to *Landmark Essays on Voice and Writing*.) For example, he maintains a kind of unhurried or relaxed directness of syntax and wording. We get some sense of reflectiveness or silence behind his words—as though he waited somewhat before speaking. His nonextreme voice tempts us to forget that this is an extreme book.

A quiet resonance also comes, I think, from a quality of discipline, order, and structure. When we try to teach with our mouth shut, the classroom conversation often wanders—or so it often happens with me. And of course Dewey is almost indelibly associated with "loose" pedagogy. But this book and the voice that speaks it is the opposite of loose. That's why the book doesn't *feel* "radical." The quality of order and discipline here is a useful antidote to half-baked or watered-down uses of Dewey.

I sense yet another dimension lying behind Finkel's voice or ethos: his deep commitment to reason, freedom, democracy, and character—goals that he manages to defend unblushingly yet utterly without naivete. I'm worried when I say this that readers will conclude that the book is corny; *corny* is the last adjective in the world to use for this book.

Let me give two examples of his matter-of-fact voice quietly telling us what is actually hard to believe.

1. He talks about the student entering the conversation with the teacher "not in a student role but as an equal." This is a wild idea to assert unless it's just a kind of sloganeering pep talk to project a generous spirit for teachers. But Finkel means it literally, and his sober and careful argument for this difficult-to-defend assertion is a good example of his point of view and of how his mind works. He acknowledges that it is indeed difficult and rare for a student to enter into conversation with the teacher as an equal. Yet he stubbornly and shrewdly argues that doing so is possible and is a goal we ought to adopt, and he suggests concrete ways to increase the chances of its happening.

2. Similarly, after he describes a perplexing problem used in teaching a concept, he says that the student has as much chance as the teacher to solve it. When I first read this assertion, again I resisted it as a kind of pious or politically correct generosity toward students. "Yeah, yeah. Students are smart. I know." (The funny thing is I actually *do* believe that all students are genuinely smart. Yet still I resisted just a bit.) "Yes," I said to myself, "this problem is a puzzle for the teacher; but

surely—speaking carefully, as Finkel tends to do—the teacher has a significantly *better* chance of solving it because of training, etc. etc. etc." Yet as I read on, I saw that he meant it literally and I had to acknowledge the strength of his careful analysis.

Is this book utopian? (Is that an indictment?) Like three other books I think of as I reflect on this one (Fishman and McCarthy; O'Reilley; Roskelly and Ronald), Finkel insists on high goals here—goals that he acknowledges no one could reach every day or even with every student over a semester. Yet the book is deeply immersed in the realities of institutional teaching and of actual teachers and students as we experience them.

Don didn't learn or work out everything in this book at Evergreen. (When Don arrived at Evergreen in 1976, I was excited to read some of the seed insights behind this book in a pamphlet he wrote with a colleague from the University of Washington—designed particularly for teachers of large lecture courses.) Nevertheless, as Don eloquently says here, Evergreen played a big role. Much of the intellectual and pedagogical richness in this book derives from Don's having taught so long in a community of fellow faculty members and students who take learning and teaching so seriously. Among the seven colleges or universities where I've taught, I've never felt such a palpable and pervasive attentiveness to the complexities of teaching and learning as I felt at Evergreen. Don wrote more about Evergreen in another book, *Educating for Freedom: The Paradox of Pedagogy* (Rutgers University Press, 1995).

Works Cited

Elbow, Peter. (1994) Introduction. *Landmark Essays on Voice and Writing.* Davis, CA: Hermagoras Press.

———. (1986) "Nondisciplinary Courses and the Two Roots of Real Learning." In *Embracing Contraries: Explorations in Learning and Teaching.* New York: Oxford University Press. Originally published as "Real Learning and Nondisciplinary Courses." *Journal of General Education* 23.2 (July 1971).

Fishman, Stephen M., & Lucille McCarthy. (1998) *John Dewey and the Challenge of Classroom Practice.* New York: Teachers College Press; and Urbana, IL: NCTE.

O'Reilley, Mary Rose. (1993) *The Peaceable Classroom.* Portsmouth, NH: Boynton/Cook.

Roskelly, Hephzibah, and Kate Ronald. (1998) *Reason to Believe: Romanticism, Pragmatism, and the Teaching of Writing.* Albany, NY: SUNY Press.

Tompkins, Jane. (1996) *A Life in School: What The Teacher Learned.* Reading, MA: Addison Wesley.

Preface

In this book I argue that our culture's image of "the great professor" is destructively narrow. The traditional "great teacher" inspires his students through eloquent, passionate speaking. He teaches by *Telling*. I use my title phrase to move beyond this restrictive notion of good teaching. Each chapter of this book illustrates a different way a teacher can teach with his mouth shut. Together, the chapters fold together to present a coherent view of teaching and learning, one that is deeply democratic in its implications.

This book is for anyone interested in education. High school and college teachers will find many approaches to teaching they may wish to try out or adapt. But the book is not intended as a manual for teachers. It aims to provoke *reflection* on the many ways teaching can be organized. It attempts to engage its readers in a conversation about education. Thus, its purpose is not so much to reform education as it is to provoke fruitful dialogue about teaching and learning among people who have a stake in education: teachers, students, parents, school administrators, policymakers, graduate students, and citizens who care about the quality of education in their nation. In addition, those who have to instruct, train, or teach as part of their job will find food for thought here. And so too will those who have had a high school or college education and wish to reflect on how that education shaped—or failed to shape—them.

Although I have kept this book fairly free of theory, the practices recounted were all shaped under the influence of philosophy and psychology. The Swiss psychologist Jean Piaget was my earliest and most profound influence. After him, my thinking has been guided by John Dewey, Jean-Jacques Rousseau, and the figure of Socrates as depicted in Plato's Socratic dialogues. I have also been strongly influenced by the psychoanalytic concept of transference as formulated by Freud, the vision of "political action" articulated by Hannah Arendt, the literacy programs of Paulo Freire, and the critique of schooling elaborated by Ivan Illich. The bibliographic note at the end includes the pertinent books by these authors.

Some readers may find it paradoxical that I attempt to undermine the notion of "teaching as Telling" by writing a book. I confront this paradox directly in Chapter 9, Conclusion. In brief, I have not written this book to change the way people think by Telling them what to think. Even if it were desirable, I do not believe you can change people's thinking this way. On the contrary, I have written it to attempt to engage you, my readers, in a conversation about education. If you reflect on what you read and formulate a response to the book, your thinking about education may change significantly. Thus, this book (or any book) does not teach through Telling. It only provides material for your mind to work over and work through.

To this end, I would urge you to read the book slowly. Don't rush through it looking for "answers" or "techniques." The book's many examples and scenes, though they are grounded in actual teaching practice, are best taken as thought-experiments. Take the time to project yourself into the situations described, and try to imagine their impact on you, as either student or teacher.

In an attempt to help make your reading of this book a reflective experience and not a didactic one, I have provided an exercise at the end: a series of questions that can be answered individually or taken as a basis for group discussion. Either way, these questions will provoke you to reflect on the book's implications and on the connections between your own educational experience and the book's central ideas. Reflecting on these questions should be considered integral to a "reading" of this book.

One of the readers of the manuscript of *Teaching with Your Mouth Shut* addressed the book's potential impact on its audience in these words:

> Of course the book is not to be taken whole cloth and used as the blueprint for educational reform. Most readers will understand this. But what is less obvious is that a conversation, or inquiry, about these ideas and practices that erupts into real classrooms could be exactly what education needs.

These words capture my hope for this book: that it will spark "a conversation . . . that erupts into real classrooms." Such a conversation would be one more example of how learning can proceed in the absence of Telling.

Acknowledgements

Driving north along the Hood Canal on Washington State Highway 101 on our way to an Evergreen College faculty retreat, my colleague Pete Sinclair and I stopped at what looked like a log cabin for lunch. Over a tasty meal, I discussed with him my several concerns and confusions about how to make the most of the sabbatical year I was anticipating the following autumn. In one or two succinct sentences, he gave me the impetus I needed to decide to write this book. He also had sage suggestions for creating the proper environment for writing it. For this advice, I thank him most gratefully.

As I finished the first draft of each chapter, I needed someone to read it to give me some sense of what I had produced. My wife, Susan Finkel, despite a busy schedule, performed this task happily, giving me not only many helpful suggestions, but also encouragement and moral support. She was at my side in more ways than I can mention from the start of this project to its finish, and without her love and help, the book would not have been completed.

I thank the following friends, colleagues, and students, who read the entire manuscript and provided me copious intelligent responses that helped me immeasurably through the stages of revision: Paul Dry, Peter Elbow, my sister Leslie Gabosh, Nancy Koppelman, Carlin Llorente, Lisa Max, Mitchell Max, Pete Sinclair, Barbara Smith, Ted Steege, and Adam Ward. In addition, my sister Gail Calder gave me useful suggestions for Chapter 1. Finally, I want to single out Mark Weisberg for time spent above and beyond the call of friendship in providing invaluable criticism and suggestions.

Stephen Monk of the University of Washington collaborated with me in developing the idea of the conceptual workshop discussed in Chapter 6 and together we devised the sequence of questions called "the Canary Problem," based on a puzzle included in James L. Adams's *Conceptual Blockbusting* (2nd ed., 1979. New York: Norton).

The ideas discussed in Chapter 8 were developed by my colleague Bill Arney and me through several years of teaching and writing together. They are more fully elaborated in our book *Educating for Freedom: The Paradox of Pedagogy* (1995. New Brunswick, NJ: Rutgers University Press). Bill has been an important colleague to me in many ways, above all in my development as an author.

I would also like to thank Sherry Walton for suggesting Heinemann as a publisher and for putting me in contact with Lois Bridges, my editor. I am grateful to Lois for her efforts in getting this book approved for publication and for removing potential obstacles that could have delayed its publication.

I had two teachers in college who not only gave me the lion's share of my education, but also sparked me to start thinking about how good teachers teach. The fact that they taught so differently was a piece of great good fortune. They are Harry Berger, Jr., and Richard J. Bernstein.

Finally, I would like to thank the faculty, staff, and students of The Evergreen State College who have provided a setting for what I have found to be a perfect vocation for myself. Above all, I thank the specific colleagues I have taught with and the specific students I have worked with. You know who you are.

TEACHING WITH YOUR MOUTH SHUT

1

—

Teaching with Your Mouth Shut

"What Do You Do?"

Meeting new people at parties, I inevitably face the question: "What do you do?" Since I am on the faculty of a liberal arts college, I could identify myself as a "professor." But I choose to take the question literally and answer by specifying an activity: I always say, "I teach college."

But if the conversation proceeds any further, I usually get uncomfortable and try to change the topic. Most people have a set of ready-made assumptions about what a teacher does. A teacher talks, tells, explains, lectures, instructs, professes. Teaching is something you do with your mouth open, your voice intoning.

This last phrase evokes an image of a boring teacher, but we think of "good teaching" simply as the artful, captivating version of the same activity (talking, telling, explaining . . .). Hence, we always hear that a teacher is like an actor, and a good class like a good theatrical performance.

Most of us *do* remember fondly those brilliant teacher/actors we may have had. After hearing their stirring lectures, we left their classrooms inspired, moved. But did we learn anything? What was left of this experience five years later? These questions usually don't get asked. Because we were touched, we felt confident that we had learned. A passionate teacher told us intellectually exciting things about her subject and we followed her line of thinking. Surely we now know something we didn't know before. Isn't this what learning consists of? In what else could it consist? What other shapes could teaching take?

1

Some teachers don't teach this way. I don't teach this way. I don't see myself as an actor. I think of myself as teaching with my mouth shut. And that is why I get uncomfortable in social conversations about my work. Other people impose on me their assumptions about teaching, and I squirm as I find myself misconstrued in this activity so central to my life.

Teaching as Telling

Our natural, unexamined model for teaching is Telling. (I capitalize the word to suggest an archetypal activity.) The fundamental act of teaching is to carefully and clearly tell students something they did not previously know. Knowledge is transmitted, we imagine, through this act of telling.

And why should we not think this way? What is wrong with this model, even granted that Telling does not always succeed? After all, if I invite a friend to dinner, and he is ignorant of the route to my house, I conquer his ignorance by *telling* him how to get there. In such a situation, telling usually works, and since knowledge has been gained in the transaction, it seems natural to use Telling as a model for teaching.

As parents, we also teach our children by telling them: We tell them that honesty is the best policy and that stealing is wrong; we tell them to put their dirty clothes in the laundry hamper and to turn down their stereos so they don't damage their hearing; we tell them they have to work hard to get ahead in life. Most of the things we want them to know, we tell them, usually over and over again. Once more, Telling seems a natural model for teaching.

Finally, what did we experience in school? If we think back to our days in the classroom, we find that we spent most of our hours either listening to a teacher talk or doing various sorts of written work at our desk. But the desk work seemed a practicing of what we learned, whereas the listening seemed the site of the actual learning. (If it wasn't our teacher telling us something, then it was the author of a textbook.) So if Telling is what teachers do when they teach, should we not take Telling as the central act of teaching?

As plausible as this conclusion seems, there are good reasons to question it. Consider the first case, telling my friend how to get to my house. It is true that I supply him with facts he did not have before. He can write my instructions down, and by adhering to them, get himself to my house. But think about the implications of using the transmission of specific information as a model for teaching. Specific information is notoriously hard to remember; that is why my friend writes my instructions down and why students who care about their grades take good notes during lectures. But transmitting information from a teacher's head to a student's notebook is an inadequate objective for education. Otherwise, we could have the teacher write the information directly in the notebook and leave the middleman (the student!) out of it.

This is why teachers give exams. They want students to take that second step and transfer the information from their notebooks into their heads in order to pass their exams. And students prove quite capable of taking this second step. But how many could pass those same exams (without any subsequent preparation) five years later? If this question seems unreasonable, ask yourself what justifies all those hours spent composing lectures, delivering them, taking notes, studying those notes, and taking exams. If all these efforts do not aim to produce any significant, *lasting* learning, then what is their point? Five years is not long to expect significant learning to last. Yet few teachers assess their own efforts (even in their imagination) by means of a "five-year standard." It seems too much to ask. But why should it be?

Educational research over the past twenty-five years has established beyond a doubt a simple fact: What is transmitted to students through lecturing is simply not retained for any significant length of time. Consult your own experience. How much do you remember from all that you were told in high school and college?

One scholar (Lion Gardiner) summarizes some of this research as follows:

> . . . research clearly favors discussion over the lecture as an instructional method when the variables studied are retention of information after a course is over, transfer of knowledge to novel situations, development of skill in thinking or problem solving, or achievement in affective outcomes, such as motivation for additional learning or change in attitudes—in other words, the kinds of learning we most care about.

Another review of the research (by D. A. Bligh) showed that lectures are "not especially effective, even for conveying content [i.e., facts]—largely because a good deal of the content presented by the instructor is not attended to by students and what is attended to may be distorted." Even if we were to accept the transmission of specific information as our goal in teaching, even if the come-to-my-house-for-dinner scenario were one we wanted to adopt as a prototype for learning, Telling would prove inadequate as our model for teaching. It is just not effective.

However, ineffectiveness is not the only reason for rejecting the instructions-to-my-house scenario. When I tell my friend how to get to my house, I allow him to solve a specific problem (how to get to my house), but I do not enrich his understanding of geography, transportation, navigation, or anything else. He doesn't have to think differently after he has digested my instructions; he has neither deepened nor broadened his understanding of the world. He simply has gained some facts he needs for a specific purpose.

We do need to learn facts about the world in order to get around in it, but absorbing specific information is not the kind of exemplary learning that ought to inspire a model of education. On the contrary, education should aim at long-lasting learning that forever alters our grasp of the world, deepening it, widening it, generalizing it, sharpening it.

When genuine understanding develops, no effort is required to retain what has been learned. A child who finally realizes that the amount of money he has in his pocket remains the same regardless of the order in which he counts the different coins must exert no effort to remember this discovery. He can never "forget" what he now understands. An adult who suddenly realizes why "I think" implies "I am" (in Descartes' famous deduction) will not forget this insight. He may develop beyond it, or transform it into a different insight, but he will require no effort to retain his new understanding of Descartes' proposition.

With some important exceptions, most teachers are not trying to get their students to learn specific information, and this is not the kind of learning we are after when we send our kids to school. What we want for them is the development of their understanding.

Unfortunately, as parents, we have not grasped that Telling is an ineffective means to stimulate understanding. So we tell our children over and over those things we think they need to understand most, even as we wonder why we have to repeat ourselves so often. No matter how many times you told her, your daughter never did learn to put her clothes in the hamper, did she? And that son of yours, always blasting his stereo, never did grasp the long-term threat to his hearing, no matter how frantically and how often you warned him.

You can tell your four-year-old son to imagine how his two-year-old sister will feel before he grabs her toy until you are blue in the face, but he will not do it. He is simply too young to put himself in his sister's place; the task is cognitively and emotionally beyond him. If he could take the step you want him to, he actually would understand the world differently: His notions of right and wrong would be deepened. But telling him to take that step is not going to get him to take it, no matter how many times you try. Telling is simply not very effective in teaching the things we care most about.

Why, then, did our schoolteachers consume so much of our childhood telling us things? Doesn't the popularity of Telling guarantee its legitimacy as a model for teaching? If the question before us were about what teachers actually do with their time, we would concede that Telling comes out on top of the list. But we are asking here about "good teaching," not just "frequent teaching," and because our experience tells us that good teaching is rare, we will not get anywhere by analyzing the most frequent cases.

By giving up on the notion that teaching at heart consists of Telling, we can begin to envisage other forms of teaching. The minute we let go of the axiom that teaching equals Telling, it is not hard to imagine alternatives.

The Great Teacher

But letting go of this fundamental equation is not easy. Everyone has been to school, and almost everyone fondly remembers a good teacher. Some may be lucky enough to have had a great teacher. What makes a teacher good, or great? In the lower grades, the teacher you fondly remember may have stood out for her nurturing qualities. But if we move to the high school years, or to college, then we are likely to fasten on a different image, one closer to our culture's image of the Great Teacher.

So let us go back to college for a moment. Let us collectively think back to that Great Teacher we had, or to the one we wistfully heard our roommate rave about. What made her so great? My guess is that, to a greater or lesser degree, she matched the following portrait.

She was enthusiastic about her subject. She seemed to know everything there was to know about it, and then some. She had an awe-inspiring command over her material, and in response to any question, could hold forth brilliantly for as long as she wished. She was captivating when she spoke. She made her field come alive. She got excited in explaining it, and her excitement was contagious. She was clear in her expositions. She asked probing questions and followed them with illuminating answers.

When her lectures were over, her students left the classroom touched by what she had said. They wished that they, too, could master this subject, or some subject. Their minds felt alive and their souls felt virtuous. They wanted to be like their teacher. They resolved to attack their books with fresh vigor, although at the back of their minds, they realized they would never be able to achieve the godlike heights she had achieved, even if they were to work at it their whole lives.

In the previous paragraphs I have been trying to capture our culture's shared image of the Great Teacher. Consider your own response to the portrait. Did it strike a chord in you? Did it make you long to be in the class of such a teacher, or to have had a like experience in your educational past? Did it evoke an ideal you carry around in the back of your mind? I think that most of my readers will answer "yes" to these questions. If so, what I have sketched quickly and with broad strokes may be said to depict our cultural ideal of good teaching.

Cultural ideals are not easy to sweep away. Images embedded in the collective experience of a culture remain deeply entrenched; we cannot give them up just because we are asked to. I have started this book by directing your attention to this ideal; my purpose in this book is to provoke you into giving it up. Teaching with your mouth shut? It sounds impossible. Surely this phrase presents a paradox. How can you possibly teach, never mind teach well, if you are barred from explaining to your students what you want them to learn? That is, indeed, the question I hope to answer.

I do not wish to disparage the captivating teacher I have sketched above, nor those teachers who aspire to be like her. I only wish to ask her to move over to make room in the spotlight for those who practice other forms of good teaching. I will concede that her teaching may be good, but only as one of many types of good teaching.

Take this Simple Test

It is almost impossible to get readers to put their book down and perform some task while they are reading. Nevertheless, I shall attempt the impossible: I would like you to stop reading this book long enough to take this simple test. Doing what I ask right now will provide you with an orientation that should prove useful in reading the rest of this book.

Find a piece of paper and a pen. Put from your mind what you have read in this book so far. Answer the following question in writing. In reflecting on this question, do not limit yourself to thinking about experiences in school. Consider the totality of your life experience.

> *Thinking back over your whole life, what were the two or three most significant learning experiences you ever had? That is, list the moments (or events) in which you discovered something of lasting significance to your life.*

Even if you can only recall one such experience, write it down. The important thing is to stop reading (at the end of this paragraph) and actually write down an answer to the question. It will only take you a few minutes. The next paragraph will still be here when you have finished writing.

Now that you have listed one, two, or three moments in your life in which you learned something that really mattered, ask yourself the following questions about each:

1. Did it take place in a classroom?
2. Did it take place in a school?

3. Was a professional teacher instrumental in making the learning experience happen?

4. Was a teacher-like figure (e.g., coach, minister, school counsellor, theater director) instrumental in making the learning experience happen?

5. If the answer to 3 or 4 is "yes," then what did the teacher (or other person) actually do to help you learn?

6. In general, what factors *were* instrumental in bringing about the learning?

Since I don't have you, my readers, all in a room together, I cannot assess the results of these questions. But when I have asked questions like these to students training to become teachers, they have been shocked at their own answers. They have found that, with only a few exceptions, most of their significant moments of learning did not take place in school and did not have teachers playing any part in them. My guess is that you found the same thing. Of course, there will be exceptions, but, after a moment's reflection, it will probably not surprise you that most people's significant learning—the learning that really matters to their lives—does not take place as a result of intentional teaching.

The reactions of some teachers-in-training to this discovery is to become discouraged. Why are they devoting their lives to teaching, if teaching is not the key to learning? But this discovery is no reason for dejection. To begin with, we achieve our most monumental forms of learning during the earliest years, before we ever set foot in a school. But even setting aside these early accomplishments, to say that most significant learning does not occur in response to teaching is not to say that significant learning *cannot* result from teaching. Who knows what teaching could accomplish if it were undertaken in the best possible manner? Perhaps, with a different kind of teaching, we could have had *more* memorable learning experiences, and perhaps, even the ones we have had would have been more profound had they been orchestrated by a master teacher.

I have asked you take my simple test for one reason only. I am convinced that most of you will discover from your answers that in those moments of learning that really mattered to you, no teacher was behaving like the brilliant lecturer of my earlier portrait. If a teacher or teacher-like figure was important to your learning, she was probably doing something different from enthusiastic Telling. I suspect she was neither charismatic nor captivating, and perhaps her most important activities were negative. Perhaps she got out of your way, gave you the opportunity to make your own mistakes, or failed to rebuke you when you expected a rebuke. But more than likely, no teacher was even present.

Good Teaching Leads to Significant Learning

Let us start, then, by characterizing "good teaching" as follows: *Good teaching is the creating of those circumstances that lead to significant learning in others.* This formulation is reasonable because it stems from the assumption that good teaching must be conceived in terms of learning. This claim seems obvious enough, yet the integral relationship between teaching and learning is easy for teachers to forget under the pressures of everyday teaching life. It is natural to assess a teaching effort either through the immediate emotional reaction it stimulates in students ("They loved me today!"), or through its fit with one's own model of "good teaching." ("Man, I gave a great lecture today!") Perhaps you did give a stellar lecture, but did anybody learn anything from it?

Our formulation reminds us of the primacy of *learning,* not teaching, in education. Learning is the end, teaching is a means to that end. Teachers must never forget that end when devising ways to teach.

The formulation does one other thing, though less flagrantly. It suggests that good teaching involves "circumstances" that lead to learning. "Circumstances" is a vague term. What does it mean? Etymologically the word refers to that which "stands around" something. In this formulation, "circumstances" refers to the conditions surrounding me as I attempt to learn. It refers therefore to the immediate *environment* of learning. A teacher's job is to shape that environment in a manner conducive to learning. A traditional way to shape a learning environment, of course, is to talk to students. But there are many other ways to design a learning environment. Some of these are more conducive to learning than a teacher's telling students what they are supposed to know.

Different Images of Good Teaching

If we can give up our entrenched image of the Great Teacher, we can start to entertain different images of good teaching. Teachers engage in a multitude of activities to help students learn. Some of them are quite surprising. These arise from conceptions of education that differ markedly from teaching as Telling. Any one of them may give us pause. From each we may learn something.

For instance, a colleague of mine, Leon, typically meets his students for discussion sessions of three or four hours at a time. The students meet to discuss an assigned literary work, and Leon listens to them talk. His sole "act of teaching" for the first two hours or more is to sit around the table with his students, listen intently to what they say, and think about what he hears. He has a notebook open in front of him, and occasionally he writes in it. Through listening to his students, he expects to improve his own understanding of the book, a book he has read many times before. Eventually, when something he has heard stimulates in him a new line of thinking about the book, he will speak, tracing out that line. If he hears nothing that leads him to new thoughts, he remains silent. But he continues to listen with fierce attention, always on the alert for the one comment that will provoke him to speak.

For students, having a respected, authoritative teacher listen with interest and concentration to their conversation about a book for several hours without speaking can be a profound experience. Leon is convinced that this is the best way he can teach literature. He also believes that the most important part of what he does lies in the listening, not in the speaking. Without going into his reasons for this conviction, and without debating whether or not he is right, we can now, I hope, consider Leon's manner of teaching intriguing. We may not agree with him, but we can see in his approach a possibility worth considering, an idea worthy of further exploration. As long as we think of great teaching only as great Telling, we cannot find Leon's conviction as anything but absurd.

I hope you will not find it absurd. Even if it seems enigmatic, I hope you will realize that Leon's silent listening, if it does nothing else, matches a condition that applied to many of your significant learning experiences: If a teacher was present, she was doing something far different from Telling. Listening intently also fulfills one additional condition: It is done with the mouth shut.

Teaching with Your Mouth Shut

"Teaching through Telling" is the phrase I am using to evoke our natural, unexamined assumptions about teaching. The phrase takes for granted that teachers teach, fundamentally and centrally, by talking—by telling students what they are supposed to know.

"Teaching with your mouth shut" is the phrase I will use to make problematic our unexamined assumptions about teaching. I intend it to suggest that there are more ways to teach well than are included in our cultural image of the Great Teacher. If we are willing to grant that teaching with your mouth shut is possible, then we must consider freshly what that activity we call teaching actually entails. From this questioning, we can build an alternative vision of teaching. And from that foundation, we can expand and diversify our notions of "great teaching." No longer will we assume that good teachers are like good actors and that great teaching entails putting on a great performance. Meeting someone at a party who admits to "teaching college," we might inquire with some curiosity how he goes about his craft, rather than assuming we already know.

If we did question him, he would likely provide some stories or some concrete descriptions of what he does in class. In what follows, I will do the same. Each chapter in this book presents a case study, a story, or a sustained image of a teaching situation—a set of "circumstances" intended to produce significant learning in students. Each is intended to make sense of the title of the book in a particular way. Each will attempt to enrich its meaning by one increment.

By the book's end I hope my phrase, "teaching with your mouth shut," will have been explored, exemplified, varied, and deepened sufficiently that it will no longer seem puzzling. "Teaching with your mouth shut" should then specify a comprehensible approach to teaching—along with a host of concrete teaching possibilities. In the end, the title phrase will, I hope, turn your head sufficiently so that not only will your notion of good teaching be transformed, but so, too, will your sense of what may be signified by the word *teaching* itself.

2

Let the Books Do the Talking

The Parable

The following little story, taken from the Gospel of Luke, was told by Jesus to his disciples. Its meaning is not obvious, yet Jesus expected them to learn something from it.

> There was once a rich man who had a manager, and he heard complaints that this man was squandering his property. So he called him in and said, "What is this I hear about you? Draw up for me an account of your management, for you can no longer be manager here." Then the manager said to himself, "What am I going to do? My master is taking my job away from me. I cannot dig; to beg I am ashamed. Ah, I know what I shall do so that, when I am removed from management, people will welcome me into their homes." Then he summoned each of his master's debtors. He said to the first, "How much do you owe my master?" "One hundred jugs of olive oil," he answered. So he said to the man, "Here, take your bond, sit down and—hurry—write it for fifty." Then he said to another, "You, how much do you owe?" He answered, "A hundred bushels of wheat." To him he said, "Here, take your bond and write it for eighty." And the master praised that dishonest manager because he had acted prudently.

Considered a great teacher even by non-Christians, Jesus often taught by means of parables—little stories pregnant with cryptic meaning. The Gospels are filled with parables, and because they are frequently incorporated into Sunday sermons, they remain in wide circulation.

Parables are by no means the exclusive property of Christians. The Hasidic rabbis of 18th-century Eastern Europe liked to tell them, too. Here is a Hasidic parable, retold by Martin Buber.

A Hasid of the Rabbi of Lublin once fasted from one Sabbath to the next. On Friday afternoon he began to suffer such cruel thirst that he thought he would die. He saw a well, went up to it, and prepared to drink. But instantly he realized that because of the one brief hour he had still to endure, he was about to destroy the work of the entire week. He did not drink and went away from the well. Then he was touched by a feeling of pride for having passed this difficult test. When he became aware of it, he said to himself, "Better I go and drink than let my heart fall prey to pride." He went back to the well, but just as he was going to bend down to draw water, he noticed that his thirst had disappeared. When the Sabbath had begun, he entered his teacher's house. "Patchwork!" the rabbi called to him, as he crossed the threshold.

Nor are parables exclusively Western. Zen Buddhist literature contains many parables. Here is one (slightly edited) from the collection, *Zen Flesh, Zen Bones*.

A beautiful Japanese girl whose parents owned a food store lived near the Zen master Hakuin. Suddenly, without any warning, her parents discovered she was with child. This made her parents angry. She would not confess who the father was, but after much harassment at last named Hakuin. In great anger the parents went to the master. "Is that so?" was all he would say.

After the child was born it was brought to Hakuin. By that time he had lost his reputation, which did not trouble him, but he took very good care of the child. A year later, the girl could stand it no longer. She told her parents the truth—that the real father was a young man who worked in the fishmarket.

The mother and father of the girl at once went to Hakuin to ask his forgiveness, to apologize at length, and to get the child back. Hakuin was willing. In yielding the child, all he said was, "Is that so?"

Native cultures also teach by telling pointed stories. The parable is a teaching device that spans all cultures and eras. (The present popularity of the books from which I have borrowed the above parables testifies to their currency today.) What is it about parables that elicits our fascination, and why have some of the world's greatest teachers relied on them?

Parables have three features in common. First, because they are little stories, they present us with specific people acting in concrete situations. Second, at least in the context of their telling, they seem profound. They appear to hold within them—waiting to be delivered—some crucial bit of wisdom or knowledge. Third, they are somewhat opaque; they do not yield their treasure too easily. We call Aesop's animal stories "fables" rather than "parables" because their point is obvious, and in case you missed it, the "moral" is spelled out and tagged onto the end. (Many of Jesus' parables seem quite obvious too, but it is clear that the majority in *his* audience did not grasp their significance.)

Learning From Parables

The three features of parables taken together reveal why they make effective teaching devices. Their concreteness, specificity, and narrative organization capture our attention. Their profundity—that they seem to signify more than simply the story itself—engages our intellect. We want to figure out what the story is "trying to tell us." So we start pondering it. Their opaqueness—that they resist easy deciphering—gives us material for reflection. Their difficulty provides grist for our mind. So these little stories become problems to be solved.

Why does the master praise his manager for releasing his debtors from some of their debt? Why is the rabbi dissatisfied with the Hasid? Why doesn't the Zen master deny the false charges leveled against him? And why does he accept the child so willingly, and then give it up so willingly? After hearing the stories, I am tempted to contemplate these questions. I have almost to make a concerted effort to avoid them. And in considering them, I will discover new questions that will either replace my initial questions or follow up on them. (For instance, why does the rabbi mock the Hasid with the specific word "patchwork"? And what is meant precisely by the question, uttered twice by Hakuin, "Is that so?")

If I begin to ponder these questions, formulate possible responses to them, test these responses against my experience and the text of the stories themselves, I have embarked upon a process of learning. I have set my mind to work to increase my understanding of the world I inhabit. And if I arrive at a conclusion that illuminates my life, then I will have learned something significant. I may even change the way I live.

I selected these three parables because I find them interesting and perplexing. I do not pretend to have grasped their wisdom, and I am not going to try to resolve them for you. But I will give you my "take" on one of them.

I first read the Zen story over twenty years ago and I have never been able to forget it. It has kept me company ever since. Its main thrust, I have concluded, is to suggest that a person may treat other people with compassion, nurturing and caring for them, without becoming attached to them. The story, I feel, insists that this is the *best* way to be connected with other people.

As a husband and father, I find this idea miraculous; it also strikes me as undesirable. Yet the parable manages to make it seem interesting, even promising. And now that I think of it, Hakuin's attitude toward the child is not so unlike my own attitude toward my students. And so the parable stays with me. I continue to muse on its mysteries. I cannot say that it has changed my life, but then my life is not yet over.

For the sake of argument, let's say that I learned something from this parable. Who taught me? Was it the Zen monk who originally made up the story, or perhaps the editor who compiled the stories and published them? But neither of these people was present to help me learn. How could either of them be taken as my teacher in any but a token sense? Doesn't it make more sense to consider the parable itself as my teacher?

In one sense it does: It is the parable that engaged my attention, provoked my thinking, and stayed with me, and from which I learned. But in another sense, calling the parable my teacher is absurd, since the parable is not human. It is nothing but marks on paper or sounds in the air; it has no agency of its own.

There is no reason we can't have it both ways. A collaboration is at work here. An anonymous Zen monk (with the help of the book's editor) places before me the text of the parable. But his teaching function stops there. If he teaches me at all, he does so simply by drawing my attention to a story. From then on, it is the story that is supposed to instruct.

But the story can't teach by itself. The story, by itself, is inert. The reader of the story, too, has to collaborate. I had to bring intellectual curiosity to the story, and I had to spend time contemplating it.

In some cases the collaboration of reader and storyteller will suffice. But most readers of this book will not seize upon one of these parables and proceed on their own to learn from it. You have enough work to consume your time and energy already. The parable alone can't convince you to take on more. And neither can I, since I am not present with you. And neither can Martin Buber, Jesus, or the monk, for the same reason.

It may take another human being who *is* present to provoke you to learn. Suppose you take a religious studies class with other adults at a neighborhood church, synagogue, or Buddhist temple. Your teacher assigns you to read one of these parables, asks you to write a short paper on what it means to you, and then discusses your paper with you. At this point we have a crucial trio of factors in the learning environment: the parable, the student, and a flesh-and-blood teacher. We can easily enrich this scene by adding the usual fourth factor: other students. In this case, the teacher will lead a class discussion on the meaning of the parable after the students have written their separate papers.

Considering this plausible scene, let's assume that some of the students learn something. We can then conclude, based on our original conception of teaching as *the creating of those circumstances that produce learning in others* (see Chapter 1), that some teaching has taken place. We do not need to debate who has done the teaching (the parable, the teacher, or even the other students) because we have already agreed that the instruction results from a collaboration. But we must underline three things: (1) The parable does not teach by Telling; it sets an engaging problem to be solved. (2) The students don't learn by listening; they learn by actively confronting the problem. (3) If the students learned by actively confronting the problem, then, most likely, the teacher did not teach by Telling. He probably did not explain the parable's meaning to the students or solve its problem for them. If he took his cues from the spirit of the parable itself, he kept the attention off himself and on the text; he provided a format within which the students could make progress; and he suggested tasks that, once undertaken, were likely to loosen the parable's knot of meaning.

Let the Parable Do the Talking

With respect to the teacher's understanding in this situation, there are two possibilities. He may think he understands the parable or he may know he does not. Either way, he can be an effective teacher. He does not have to fathom the parable's meaning to be useful to his students. He may even be better off if he doesn't, for then he won't be tempted to rob the students of their own struggle.

If he does think he grasps the meaning of the parable, he should be careful not to convey it to the students for two reasons: (1) These stories have lived for centuries; they have not been solved once and for all. One of his students may discover an even more satisfying interpretation of the parable than his own. Conveying his own interpretation would prevent this important event from happening. (2) If people could learn what the parable has to teach through being told its meaning, then the parable never would have been invented in the first place! *The existence of the parable as a teaching device presumes that certain things can be learned only by figuring them out for yourself.* So the teacher should teach with his mouth shut. He may speak in order to guide his students in their learning activities, but he should "let the parable do the talking."

I have dwelt on parables for so long because they compress and simplify a teaching process that can take place at greater length and in more complex form with certain books. Since my concern is not with the teaching of spiritual or religious wisdom but rather with the kind of teaching that is appropriate to our high schools and colleges, I am not interested in parables for their own sake. But they make a telling exemplar: We can transfer what we have learned from examining them to teaching with other kinds of material.

Puzzles and Paradoxes

Before I move on to books, the main subject of this chapter, let me say a word specifically about the teaching of math and science. For the kind of learning that centers on numbers or the physical world rather than human relationships, there exists something very like the parable, and that is the puzzle, paradox, or perplexing problem. The following example deals with some elementary concepts in physics. After you read it, take a moment to think about it.

> A canary is standing on the bottom of a very large sealed bottle that is placed on a scale. The bird takes off and flies around the inside of the bottle. What happens to the reading of the scale? Explain.

We would not call this perplexing question a parable, but it has features very close to the same three that characterize parables. (1) Although it has too minimal a narrative structure to be called a story, it is, like a story, concrete and engaging. (2) It may not have the scent of wisdom about it, but it clearly has an answer, and it is sufficiently intriguing to make us curious about the answer. (3) Finally, it does not yield its treasure easily. It is challenging. As long as you exclude professional physicists, you can generate a lively and heated conversation among almost any group of adults by posing this question.

Almost everything in our discussion about how the parable teaches applies also to the puzzle. The puzzle can provoke learning by itself, but is more likely to teach effectively in collaboration with a live teacher and a group of students who can talk to each other. A teacher who teaches "in the spirit of the puzzle" will not give the answer, lecture on the reasons for it, or rob students of an opportunity to solve it on their own. He will keep himself in the background and let the puzzle do the talking.

I stress the structural similarity between puzzles and parables to emphasize that the discussion which follows, though it centers on learning in the humanities, can be applied (with some modification) to learning in the social and natural sciences and in mathematics. (See Chapter 6 for amplification.) But let me also caution that no instance of teaching discussed in this book is intended to present a universal model for teaching. None is meant to stand alone in the teaching of even one subject, and certainly none is intended to suffice for the teaching of all subjects.

Teaching through Great Books

A great piece of literature like *The Brothers Karamazov* plunges you into a world different from your own, yet one which also resembles your world in important ways. The book opens up perplexing questions that matter to you. In *The Brothers Karamazov* some of these questions are explicitly presented. For instance, the "Grand Inquisitor" chapter asks whether the gift of freedom eradicates happiness from human life. In other books the questions are implicit, arising between the lines. Nonetheless they are vital to the book's power. And a great book will tender its questions so they are difficult to avoid. Whether a novel, a poem, or a play, the work will advance its questions in concrete, often dramatic, form. It will make them compelling. We are invited to enter the fray and respond.

The three features of parables apply to great works of literature as well. Great books are concrete and engaging, they are profound, and they are opaque, requiring work to understand them. But instead of posing one problem, a great book poses sequences of related problems, or nests of problems within problems. We cannot concentrate our energies all on one specific knot; rather we have to locate the various knots, work out their relationships to each other, and think about them both separately and together. We are faced with a more complex process of problem solving, but in spirit we have not left the world of the parable.

Thus, a teacher does well to assign *The Brothers Karamazov* and let his students confront the book directly. He can do the same with many great works of literature, and of philosophy and history, too. By looking at one of these in some detail, and several others briefly, we can come to see why teachers need not stand between their students and the book. They can step to one side and trust the book to awaken their students' minds. The better the book, the more the teacher can keep his own mouth closed.

But he will not stand back and do nothing. He will provide structure and activities to help his students attend carefully to the book, learn what is necessary about its setting and language, actively respond to its perplexities, and draw on each other in making sense of the story. "Teaching with your mouth shut" does not entail teacher passivity; it requires different *kinds* of activities from teachers. In examining how great books stimulate learning, we must be mindful that there are many ways teachers can help students read these books carefully and enter deeply into the conversations engendered by their reading. (See Chapters 3 through 8 for many examples.)

In what follows I shall consider six examples, one at length. I have not chosen them randomly or casually; they are all great works of literature. In suggesting that one way to teach with your mouth shut is to let the books do the talking, I do not mean that any old book will do. Most books do not have profound enough things to say, nor do they "speak" in interesting enough ways for a teacher to lean so heavily on them. It is necessary to seek out exceptional books.

Homer's *Iliad*

The *Iliad* is a long epic poem, with its roots in an oral tradition of tale telling; it is the earliest written work still existing from the world of ancient Greece. The *Iliad* depicts a series of events lasting about two weeks during the ninth year of the Trojan War.

The Trojan War was launched by the Greeks against Troy to take back Helen, Queen of Sparta and wife to King Menelaus. Helen had allowed herself to be abducted by a Trojan prince and taken off to Troy to live as his wife. Greece at this time consisted of a collection of tiny kingdoms, each the size of a town or island, each independent and autonomous, each ruled by its own king. Menelaus was simply one of these kings. His brother, Agamemnon, was another, as were Odysseus and Achilles, to name only a few of the Greek heroes.

After Helen was abducted, Agamemnon assembled an army from among the Greek kingdoms and sailed to Troy (located on the coast of what is now Turkey). His "army" actually consisted of many separate armies, each led by its own king. Thus, Odysseus commanded the Ithacans, Menelaus the Spartans, and Achilles the Myrmidons, while Agamemnon, as well as leading his own Mycenaeans, also commanded the other kings. Or at least he tried to; his difficulty in doing so is what the *Iliad* is all about.

As the *Iliad* starts, the war has been going on for nine years. Though the Greeks were superior in arms to the Trojans, every victory on the battlefield culminated in the Trojans' retreat behind the invincible walls of the city. No matter how successful the Greeks were on the battlefield outside of Troy, these successes got them no closer to Helen, secured inside the city.

One might wonder why the Greeks fought on for nine years under these conditions. The answer is that Helen was only one of the prizes for which they were fighting—the pretext for the war, but not the only incentive. The Greeks were also fighting for the highly valued prizes of glory and booty. Glory they derived from victory in face-to-face individual combat with illustrious Trojan aristocrats. (The greatest possible glory would come from killing the greatest Trojan warrior—Hector.) Booty they got from their incessant raids on the surrounding towns and villages, as well as from the weapons and armor they stripped from defeated Trojans, and the wealth given them as ransom for prisoners of war. In addition to material wealth, their booty consisted of women seized from conquered villages and taken as concubines.

Chryseis, the daughter of a local priest of Apollo, had been captured by Agamemnon. At the story's start, Agamemnon is forced to return Chryseis to her father in order to end a plague among his armies caused by Apollo. Agamemnon is not happy about giving up his prize. He agrees to do so only because his fellow kings insist on it, but like a spoiled schoolboy, he makes up his loss by seizing a similar spoil of war from a companion. Unfortunately for the Greeks, he chooses the wrong companion — the great warrior, Achilles. He demands from Achilles his newly acquired concubine, Briseis. Insulted and outraged, Achilles comes close to drawing his sword and slaying Agamemnon. In the end, he yields, giving up Briseis, but at the same time deciding in anger to withdraw his army from the war effort. He storms off from Agamemnon's tent vowing not to fight no matter how bad things got for the Greeks. "You will eat your heart out . . . for this dishonor," he tells Agamemnon.

The *Iliad* goes on to recount the devastating consequences of Achilles' withdrawal from the war. While Trojans are slaughtering Greeks and trying to burn their boats, Achilles lolls about his tent, enjoying the company of his beloved friend Patroclus, playing the lute and singing songs. After much havoc, Agamemnon relents and tries to get Achilles to change his mind by righting the wrong he did to him. But despite being offered an apology, the return of his concubine, and much more besides, Achilles refuses to fight. Only later, after Patroclus is slain on the battlefield by Hector, does an angry Achilles finally enter the war. This time his anger is directed at Hector, whom he eventually humiliates and kills.

Does the Iliad Glorify War?

The *Iliad* is rich in drama, passion, grief, and joy. After reading it, one is left with many questions. A list of issues raised by the text (which runs for nearly 600 pages in the Robert Fitzgerald translation) would be long indeed. Rather than attempt such a list, I am going to single out only two questions raised by the poem. I want to illustrate what it could mean to "let the book do the talking" when the book in question is the *Iliad*.

The most pressing question for me, the one I simply cannot avoid, is whether the poem glorifies war, or whether, on the contrary, it makes the most compelling case imaginable *against* war. This question presses itself on me because the poem seems to do both, and to do both with immense power.

When I said that the Greeks came to Troy to win glory, I did not do justice to this motive. The quest for glory in battle dominates the *Iliad*. Aristocratic soldiers seek each other out on the battlefield, question each other as to identity and pedigree, and hurl insults at each other in almost ritualized verbal warfare before seeking to bring each other down in blood. Homer spares us none of the details of these encounters and he presents them endlessly. He never tires of recounting the personal battles between two individuals, one Greek and one Trojan, for in these encounters lies the meaning of ancient warfare. What happens during those moments renders the war *memorable,* worthy of recounting as a tale many centuries afterwards.

In some encounters the Trojan warrior is victorious, in others the Greek. It doesn't seem to matter to Homer. What matters to him is the fight itself: the pitting of character against character, skill against skill, the high passion, the need to win, the stakes, the glory won or lost, the *name* a man made for himself through the defeat of someone else with an honorable name.

There is no question that the poem glorifies war. Listen to Hector as he rallies the Trojan allies upon seeing the wounded Agamemnon withdraw from the battlefield.

> "Trojans, Lykians, and Dardan spears
> remember valor, friends, and fight like men.
> Their champion has left the field! Oh, here,
> here is my great chance, granted me by Zeus!
> Now forward with your teams into the center
> and win the highest prize of all!"
>
>   He stirred them,
> rallying each man's courage. As a hunter
> would send his hounds against a lion or boar
> so Hector sent his Trojans headlong in
> against the Akhaians: Hector, Priam's son
> hard as the wargod—now in pride and zeal
> this hunter led his fighters on. He fell
> on the battle line like a high screaming squall
> that blows down on the purple open sea!
> And who were the adversaries that he killed
> when Zeus accorded him this rush of glory?
> Asaios first, Autonoos and Opites,
> Dolops Klytides, Opheltios, Agelaos,
> Aisymnos, Oros, rugged Hipponoos—
> these leaders of Danaans he destroyed,
> then turned on the rank and file. . . .

Notice the stress on the names of the defeated aristocratic Greek warriors. Each is an individual man of importance; the distinctive name of each adds one more increment to Hector's glory. And just as important, each dead man is immortalized by having his name recorded in Homer's song.

The poem is littered with descriptions like the one above. Homer puts us on the battlefield alongside these warriors and he makes us feel what moved them. We may personally hate violence, but when we hear the words of Hector as he rallies his troops like a pack of hunting hounds, when we sense the kind of personal glory a valiant warrior could attain, we begin to understand the ancient human attraction to warfare.

But if the *Iliad* glorifies war, it equally reveals its horror and absurdity. Consider this passage.

> Then Meges killed
> Pedaios, bastard son of Lord Antenor,
> a son whom Lady Theano had cherished
> equally with her own, to please her husband.
> Meges Phyleides, the master spearman,
> closing with him, hit his nape: the point
> clove through his tongue's root and against his teeth.
> Biting cold bronze, he fell into the dust.

Such descriptions occur again and again in the poem. In so few lines, and at the same time that he is glorifying the victor's victory, Homer forces us to feel the pain of the defeated man.

We are confronted with the unmitigated brutality of violent killing. There are no clean deaths in the *Iliad*. Each one is anatomically vivid and physiologically repulsive. ("Through bronze and bone/the spearhead broke into the brain within/and left it spattered. Down he went.") We shudder as we read. Homer does not allow us to fool ourselves for a minute about the nature of death in war. He gives us no easy deaths; he puts the gore directly before us. Even as he glorifies war, he is mercilessly honest about what he is glorifying.

And that is not all. We are forced not just to confront the physical horror of men hacking each other to pieces with crude metal weapons; we are also forced to feel the mother's pain at the loss of her son, the young man's regret at a life prematurely extinguished, the wife's grief for a slain husband who will never return to meet his infant son, the father's anguish at losing two sons at once ("he took their lives,/leaving their father empty pain and mourning—/never to welcome them alive at home/after the war, and all their heritage/broken up among others").

Homer compresses these descriptions of death so effectively that we feel everything at once: the thrill at the glory won in taking a life, the horror at the waste of life taken, the pleasure in the prowess of the spear-thrower, the pain in the destruction inflicted by the spear. Over and over, the contradictions at the center of war come to life as we read, and they do not resolve themselves.

What the Iliad Teaches about War

The *Iliad* does not teach us that war is good, nor does it teach that war is bad. *It teaches both at the same time.* It doesn't preach either proposition; it presupposes both, and goes on to make each a compelling truth for its readers. Yet each of these propositions would seem to flatly contradict the other. How can we possibly accept them both?

This is one of the profound questions the *Iliad* puts before us. The poem invites us to ponder this question, to open up a line of inquiry about it. It provokes us to discuss this question with our friends, to consider it in the context of our own life and times, to examine our own responses to anger, violence, and death.

The *Iliad* offers no answer to this question—no easy way out. But it does offer us an education. We can educate ourselves by taking the question seriously and undertaking to pursue it with others.

As we do so, we may discover other compelling questions that turn up as we proceed. Pursuing them may aid us in our original inquiry. Or a new quest may render the original one obsolete. Eventually, we may arrive at our own response to the poem's perplexing attitude toward war.

If we arrive at a response that is faithful both to the text and to our own experience, then we will have learned something important from our study of the *Iliad*. We will have deepened our grasp of the human world we inhabit. We will have taken a step in our education.

A teacher may help us respond to the *Iliad* by providing useful classroom formats for discussion, by assigning papers which force us to articulate our thinking clearly and rigorously, by assigning illuminating readings about other wars, and in many other ways. But a teacher will not be able to answer the *Iliad*'s questions for us. A teacher who tries to will only make himself an obstacle to our education. And a teacher who thinks he understands the real truth about war is unlikely to be able to offer us anything in his own words to rival what Homer has given us in his. The best thing he can do is make the *Iliad* available to us and "let Homer do the talking."

A Telling Silence

The first question I have discussed arises from a quality of the poem that pervades the whole: Homer's manner of depicting warfare. The second question, by contrast, arises at one specific moment during the story, and by means of a telling silence.

Recall that when Agamemnon realizes he cannot do without Achilles, he tries to persuade him to drop his grudge. In Book 9 of the *Iliad*'s 24 Books (chapters), Agamemnon sends three emissaries to Achilles' tent to apologize and to offer him copious recompense for his insult: seven new tripods, ten bars of gold, twenty shining cauldrons, twelve thoroughbred horses, seven beautiful women "deft in household craft," *and* his own cherished Briseis, accompanied by a solemn oath that Agamemnon "never went to bed or coupled with her,/as custom is with men and women." In addition, Agamemnon offers much, much more to be delivered after their victory over Troy. Each of the three delegates also makes his own personal heartfelt appeal. For the good of all, Achilles must take up his sword again.

At this point, readers expect Achilles to be delighted. He has "taught Agamemnon a lesson," gotten his revenge, and the wrong done him is about to be completely reversed. We cannot imagine that Achilles will refuse. After all, he has come to Troy to fight, to win back Helen, and to gain eternal glory. He can attain none of these objectives without reentering the battle. His deepest original motives, the righting of the wrong done to him, the multiple assuagements offered by Agamemnon, and the persuasive appeals of his friends all taken together would seem to leave nothing lacking to lead him back to war.

And yet he refuses. No one in the Greek army could be more astonished at this response than we are as we read. To make matters worse, Achilles offers no reason for his refusal. He does give a series of speeches in response to the emissaries, but he says nothing in these speeches that explains his continued refusal to fight. He merely reiterates his original injury and re-expresses his original anger. We are left wondering whether even he knows the reasons for his present refusal. But whether he does or not, he does not vacillate for even a moment. His response is decisive, unambiguous, and resolute.

Why Does Achilles Refuse to Fight?

Why, at this point and under these circumstances, does Achilles persist in his refusal to fight? You cannot read the *Iliad* without running smack up against this question. And the poem provides no answer. You can read the scene over and over, and you can read all the way through the following fifteen books to the poem's end, and still you will not find an answer. You will only discover the circumstances that lead Achilles to change his mind in a burst of passion—the death at Hector's hand of his dearest friend, Patroclus.

But though you cannot avoid the question, and you cannot easily answer it, you also cannot brush it aside. The poem points to the importance of this question just as surely as it does not answer it.

The *Iliad,* let us recall, is about anger. Its very first line announces this theme ("Anger be now your song, immortal one"). The *Iliad* provides a penetrating analysis of the necessary yet unstable relationship between anger and warfare. This problematic connection comes alive in the figure of the enraged warrior who will not fight, an enigma we cannot ignore.

"Anger Be Now Your Song"

A warrior society like that of the Greeks had to value anger highly because it was anger that fueled the passions of men and led them to fight. Each army's commander (as Homer shows in the poem) had to kindle the anger of his men in order to raise them to their fighting best. In an age of minimal technology, straightforward military strategy, and conventionalized modes of combat, the rousing of the spirits of his warriors by word and example was a commander's most important duty.

A man with a fierce temper, like Achilles, should make an ideal warrior. And so he did, as long as his brilliant anger stayed focused on his enemies. But anger is not an easily directed passion. A man quick to anger may just as readily rage at a friend as at an enemy. He may even turn against his own commander. And a man who turns against his commander does not make a good soldier. An army made of up of volatile, enraged men does not hold together well. It is not the kind of army you would want to lead.

The *Iliad* makes us aware of the uneasy relation between successful warfare (under ancient conditions) and the emotion upon which it rests, and this awareness prevents us from brushing aside the question of why Achilles refuses to fight after the generous offers and persuasive appeals of Book 9.

A Witness to War

The story's opening depicts not only the events that enraged Achilles but also the childlike quality of his anger. Insulted by Agamemnon, he "takes his marbles and goes home." He then appeals successfully to his mother, Thetis, a minor goddess with good connections to Zeus, to intervene with the major gods who are influencing the war behind the scenes. At Achilles' urging, she pleads with Zeus to turn the tide of war against the Greeks so that Achilles' withdrawal will be painfully regretted. And Zeus, who has always had a soft spot in his heart for Thetis, accedes. The war turns, the Trojans get the upper hand, and the Greeks suffer death, devastation, and demoralization.

Achilles has done all he can to make sure that his tormentor is punished. But inadvertently he has brought about a surprising change of circumstance for himself. *He has made himself a witness to war.*

Rarely, if ever, has a man whose defining virtue is excellence in combat brought himself to the site of war and willingly and willfully sat by and failed to fight. It is crucial to the story that Achilles does not take his men and go home. He stays on the fields of Troy, at the periphery of the battleground, where he remains inactive. We can only wonder what is going through his mind as the battle rages around him. Homer does not tell us. Yet the thoughts and feelings of the witness to war must be responsible for his shocking and enigmatic refusal to fight.

Through the most unexpected sequence, Achilles' anger has led to his passivity. True, this condition is temporary, but it is weighty nonetheless. Homer has no choice but to eventually return Achilles to the bloody battle-field; Achilles must kill Hector and turn the tide of battle—that is his destiny, and the story is too well-known for Homer to alter it, even if he wanted to.

But Homer takes his time in bringing Achilles to his glory. He does not return Achilles to combat until Book 20, more than three-quarters of the way through the poem. Reading a poem whose protagonist is the greatest warrior of his age and whose theme appears to be the glory of combat, the reader cannot but pause over the glaring fact that Homer devotes seventy-nine percent of his poem to *keeping Achilles from the battlefield.* He has to ask why. He has to inquire into Achilles' condition. He has to try, somehow, to untangle the knot that Homer has thrust into his hands. Maybe witnessing war without actually participating in it alters Achilles' perspective.

Making Connections, Going Deeper

The two questions I have discussed are not buried deeply in the poem; they strike most readers immediately. They also seem connected.

Achilles does not withdraw from the war because he has come to question the goodness or badness of war, he withdraws to punish Agamemnon. But his refusal to re-engage in battle may derive from a dawning awareness of the problematic nature of war. There is no direct evidence to support this interpretation, but it is hard to avoid linking Achilles' protracted refusal to fight with some kind of judgment about war. Homer goes to great lengths to make sure we can't attribute Achilles' refusal to its original cause; he undoes all the causes of injury that Achilles suffered from Agamemnon, and more than that, he overcompensates for them by means of Agamemnon's generous offers. So what is left?

A decision about action almost always rests on a judgment, and Achilles' decision is not to fight. This decision may rest on some new judgment about fighting—a judgment so new to him, and so unformed, that he cannot put it into words. That would explain his inability to justify his continued refusal to Agamemnon's delegation, friends he has no desire to disappoint or frustrate.

The above interpretation is made more likely by the dual quality in Homer's depiction of individual combat that we have already examined. If the fighting that we witness as we read forces upon us a contradictory assessment of war, if it makes us question the ethical value of fighting, then it may do the same for the other witness to the war, Achilles.

The two questions we have examined, if pursued far enough, make contact with each other. In a great work such as the *Iliad*, all important questions will be related. Part of the work's greatness derives from its unity, its artistic integrity, its having been crafted as a whole. Therefore, as diverse as the problems and questions may appear, we will always find, if we work hard enough, some deeper level at which we can make important connections among them. Offering this potential for making connections, and hence for going deeper into the text, is another way in which great books promote our education. They do not ultimately provoke scattered and separate inquiries; rather they lead us into a unified and therefore more profound search. We do not become divided and distracted as we pursue their various strands of meaning; rather we become more focused, and finally more whole.

A Caution

The length of the preceding discussions of but two questions from the *Iliad* may create some misleading impressions about what is required of a teacher who would "let Homer do the talking." My readers may feel that I am implying that a teacher must have a detailed and finished interpretation of a great book before he can step back and let his students confront the perplexities of the book directly. Nothing could be further from my intent.

Of course, teaching in this manner does not require any less preparation time on the teacher's part. He will need to read the book carefully, being open to his own responses in order to discover what genuine, living questions it raises for him. But by no means should he feel compelled to come to class with fully worked-out answers to these questions. Our discussion of parables made it clear that the teacher who knows he does not have the answer is often the one who can be most useful to students in their encounter with puzzling and meaningful texts. I have spent so many words on the *Iliad* because I wanted to show how a great book raises serious questions for its readers, because I wanted to show how apparently diverse questions connect as one probes deeper, and finally because I have an abiding fascination with the work itself.

Other Examples

I have examined one text at some length in order to give the flavor of how great books can educate without the need of "translation" by a teacher. In what follows, I will comment on several more books I could just as well have used as my leading example. For each I include just one of many questions that a careful reading brings to life. Confronting any of these questions can lead to an education.

Ancient Greek works dominate my list because I have used them often in my own teaching. But my list should in no way suggest that I am making an argument for the exclusive use of the traditional Western canon in general, or ancient texts in particular. Virginia Woolf's and Joseph Conrad's best books could easily be added, as could Hawthorne's and Melville's. So could Lady Murasaki's *Tale of Genji*, a book as great as any in the Western tradition. Each teacher has to make his own list. I have selected some of the great books I know best.

1. Sophocles' *Oedipus the King* does not depict, as is often thought, a man who accidentally kills his father and marries his mother. Rather this tragedy depicts a man *gradually discovering* that he has carried out these deeds (before the action of the play begins!) and that he is therefore responsible for the plague that has fallen on his people. It is a play in which an important man discovers—to his horror—who he really is.

   This play explores the difficult relationship between the human desire for self-knowledge and the gods' commandment to be reverent, obedient, and wary of seeking to cross the limits that naturally circumscribe the human condition, limits that separate men and women from the gods. Even as we admire Oedipus for his steadfast search for the truth, we must ask whether he was wise to persist so relentlessly in the face of ominous warnings. We are forced, finally, to question the human desire for knowledge—the very impulse that would seem to make humans noble.

2. Thucydides' *Peloponnesian War* provides a vivid account of the war between Athens and Sparta (431–404 B.C.) and of the political deliberations that led to Athens' disastrous military policy in conducting this war. Thucydides not only puts before us suspenseful battle scenes with discussions of military strategy, but presents compelling re-creations of the public debates in the Athenian assemblies where decisions on how to conduct the war were reached. As we listen to one persuasive

speaker after another arguing for opposing courses of action, we find ourselves drawn in, trying to decide how we, ourselves, would have voted, had we been present. Because the speakers are so effective, the prudent and wise course of action in any instance is never obvious to the reader. It is only in retrospect, as the story unfolds, that he can look back and either praise or condemn himself for his hypothetical vote.

In reading Thucydides, we are forced to examine the fragile and vulnerable nature of political decision making under a democracy, and ultimately to question the value of democracy for a great nation at war. The radically democratic nature of Athens' way of life seems responsible both for her greatness and her downfall. How, finally, are we to judge democracy under the shadow of the tragic story Thucydides recounts?

3. Plato's Socratic dialogues present us with the enigmatic and captivating character of Socrates. To what degree this portrait is historically accurate and to what degree fictional, we will never know. In these dialogues, Socrates engages in conversations with one or several people (but always one at a time) about philosophical questions. Many are about the nature of particular virtues such as courage, moderation, and justice. Others confront educational questions: whether virtue can be taught, or what kind of knowledge is possessed by teachers of rhetoric—persuasive speech that enabled citizens to succeed in the law courts and political councils of Athens.

If you read one of these dialogues, you will of course encounter the philosophical question that is the topic of that dialogue. And if you read a number of these dialogues together, you will confront a number of philosophical questions related to each other. But over and above these questions (or perhaps, beneath them), you will be forced to face a different set of questions: What is Socrates trying to do by his peculiar manner of carrying on a conversation? What are we to make of the many contradictions that surround his actions and speech? What is the significance of his whole life, and of his death (he was executed at age 70 for corrupting the youth of Athens)? The character of Socrates (in both senses of the word) presents one huge question, a question that cannot be avoided by those who read a number of these dialogues together. And readers soon discover that the question about Socrates the man is not unrelated to the philosophical questions Socrates pursues in conversation. In responding to the latter, you are gradually "seduced" into responding to Socrates the man.

4. Any of Shakespeare's great plays could serve as my next example; *Julius Caesar* will do as well as any. The play might be better titled "The

Tragedy of Brutus," for Brutus is the protagonist and the play centers on his decision to join a conspiracy to assassinate Julius Caesar and on the events that follow the assassination, leading eventually to Brutus' defeat and suicide. By the play's end, the reader (or viewer) must wonder why Brutus joined in this murder. At first Brutus is torn; yet he quickly allows himself to be persuaded by Cassius to join the conspiracy. An astute and intelligent man, Brutus disappoints us with his paltry rationale:

> It must be by his death; and for my part,
> I know no personal cause to spurn at him,
> But for the general. He would be crowned.
> How that might change his nature, there's the question.
>
>   . . .
>
>   to speak truth of Caesar,
> I have not known when his affections swayed
> More than his reason. But 'tis a common proof
> That lowliness is young ambition's ladder,
> Whereto the climber upward turns his face;
> But when he once attains the upmost round
> He then unto the ladder turns his back
> Looks in the clouds, scorning the base degrees
> By which he did ascend. So Caesar may;
> Then lest he may, prevent. (I.iii.10–28)

It doesn't take long, in the wake of the murder, for Brutus to doubt his deed and eventually regret his decision. So why did this seasoned, wise, and intelligent man allow himself to be persuaded to so extreme an act by a shallow man whose motives were both egotistical and transparent? In asking ourselves this question, a question for which the play gives no ready answer, we are forced to face a deeper question: Do we ever grasp the reasons for our own actions? This question touches us to the heart, because even in our post-Freudian age, it is difficult to answer and even more difficult to ignore; answering it seems crucial to our identity as the species that defines itself as "a rational animal" (Aristotle).

5. Toni Morrison's *Beloved* tells the story of a haunting. The ghost of a murdered child returns to the home of its mother, a former slave living in Cincinnati who killed her beloved daughter rather than see her returned to slavery under the terms of the Fugitive Slave Act. The book dramatizes the struggle of "freed" people trying to live a life that is not totally dominated and destroyed by their enslaved past. In part, this is

a problem of memory: what to do with the inhuman memories of a brutalized life? The ghost serves as a metaphor for these memories, and it threatens to completely engulf the mother's current life. *Beloved* makes its readers ask whether a former slave can possibly transform herself into a free woman after she has lived through the unthinkable events that slavery brought upon herself, her family, and her community. This question has reverberations that go all the way back to Exodus and a contemporary urgency for both white and black Americans, each of whom still struggles to live together in the wake of the slavery that one group imposed upon the other.

Let the Books Do the Talking

When I get a group of students to read the *Iliad,* or *Julius Caesar,* or *Beloved,* and when I arrange things so that they will pay good attention to the book, read it with the whole of their being, as it were, and respond back to it in the same way, then I am "letting the book do the talking." Trusting the book to move the students and the students to become curious about what moves them, I refrain from explaining the book's significance to them. In this sense, I "keep my mouth shut." I do not create a classroom organized around my own speech. Rather, I create a classroom energized by the sparks created when students and book rub up against each other.

Just selecting the right book is the first step, and not a trivial step by any means. Getting the students to read it is the second step, and the third is "arranging circumstances" so that students read it well, opening themselves up to the book and working to examine its significance. I lump together the two activities of paying attention to the book and responding back to it because reading well necessitates both. The teacher's job, then, is to select the book wisely, to get the students to read it, and to get them to read it well.

I have said all I can about selecting wisely. Getting students to read the book is usually not that hard, since most teachers work in an institution that surrounds learning with the trappings of coercion. It is getting the students to read *well* that tests the teacher's art. I have alluded only briefly to this challenge in this chapter, but virtually every chapter that follows bears directly on it. The connections with this chapter will be apparent because the majority of my examples and scenarios center around students learning from great books.

In this chapter, then, I have focused primarily on "the books" and only indirectly on getting the students to attend carefully and respond to those books. I *have* tried, however, never to let the reader forget the necessity of those correlative teaching activities. My main effort has been, nevertheless, to convince you that some books can provide students an education without a teacher's explaining what they mean.

3

Let the Students Do the Talking

Discussing a Book with Others Who Have Read It

In the last chapter I argued that students can learn from great books, if they read them carefully. In this chapter I will argue that teachers can develop the discipline of careful reading by organizing their classrooms as seminars where students struggle to understand a book through mutual discussion—without an Expert's telling them what it means.

"Where Shall We Start?"

Let us picture a class of high school seniors discussing the first three books of the *Iliad* in a World Literature course. Twenty-five students and a teacher meet around a table. The teacher, Ms. Green, occupies no special seat at the table; like the students she takes a different chair each day. Sunshine penetrates the large windows, lighting up the room. A large chalkboard takes up one wall.

As the hour strikes, Ms. Green looks down at a sheet of paper, and says, "Laura, it's your turn to go to the board." Laura advances to the chalkboard. "Who has questions today?" she asks. The students rustle through their notebooks. Hands begin to shoot in the air. Laura points to Jennifer.

"Are we supposed to believe that the gods in the *Iliad* are real?"
Laura writes on the board: "1. Gods real??—(Jennifer)"
"They must be," pipes up Joe, "because . . . ," but Ms. Green cuts him off.
"Let's get all the questions up before we try to answer them."
Laura points to another raised hand: "Mark?"

31

"Why are the Greeks fighting this war? Are they really willing to spend ten years so far away from home just for a woman? There must be another reason." Laura writes: "2. Real reasons for the war?—(Mark)" As the questions go up, most students write them down in their notebooks. So too does Ms. Green. Lisa asks why Homer spends so much of Book 2 listing the soldiers and the number of ships in each army. "It was *so* boring!" she says. Ms. Green scribbles a note to herself to answer this question when the time is right.

Laura calls on each raised hand. Some students refer to a specific passage, mentioning the page number, and when they do, Laura writes the page number on the board with the question.

After ten minutes no hands remain in the air. Laura asks the class, "OK, where do you want to start?" Brett suggests the first question. Jessica suggests they should address the "picky" question about Achilles' background "to get it out of the way." John suggests "the reasons for the war," arguing that a decent answer will help them with three or four other questions on the board. There is a murmur of approval, and Laura says, "That sounds good. Let's begin there. Mark, that's your question. Say a little more about it?" Laura then takes her seat.

Mark rephrases his question and explains why he raised it. He just can't believe so many men would be willing to leave their wives and children for so long just to force an unwilling wife to return to her husband. "But Helen wasn't just a wife," exclaims Jennifer. "She was a queen."

"And besides, she was the most beautiful woman in the world!" says Brett.

"These guys don't care about Helen," says Jim. "They just love to fight. They're having a great time. Helen was just an excuse."

And so the conversation begins. The class period will go by quickly. By the time the bell rings, most of the questions on the board will remain unaddressed and none will be fully answered. But some light will have been shed on two or three or four of them.

To Struggle on Their Own

Ms. Green made a note to answer the question about the boring catalogue of ships in Book 2 because she thought it a reasonable question and she believed the students would have no way to answer it based on the text. But for the moment she holds her tongue, trusting that a proper time will come, if not during the discussion, then tomorrow, when she can steal five minutes from a different class activity she has planned.

She will not wrest the initiative from the students who already are engaged in heated discussion about the reasons for the war. "The seminar," she reminds herself, "belongs to the students. I have other places in the course to provide background information. This is the time for them to struggle with the text on their own." And so she holds off her five-minute explanation of how epic poetry was the only way for oral cultures to preserve a record of "who was there" and "what they did."

The Seminar

Seminar is a long-established term in education, yet it is ambiguous and covers a variety of circumstances. Three common seminars are: (1) the graduate-style seminar in which students present formal papers to their peers and receive questions and criticism in response, (2) the (misnamed) Socratic seminar in which a teacher leads her students to a preordained conclusion through carefully formulated questions and the deft art of conversation management, and (3) the open-ended seminar to which students bring their own questions (about some topic or reading) and in which, through conversation and inquiry, they address some of these questions. While each version has a legitimate rationale, the third is the most removed from Telling; in the open-ended seminar, the teacher "lets the students do the talking."

The Open-Ended Seminar

There are many ways to run an open-ended seminar, but its governing principles remain constant. They are implicit in Ms. Green's restraint and in what we have seen so far of her class.

1. The purpose of the seminar is for the students to deepen their understanding of something they have already examined: a book, a chapter, an article, a film, a play, a lecture delivered previously, or any potentially educational experience from the recent past (e.g., lab, field trip, political event).

2. *The outcome of the seminar must not be predetermined;* the seminar must really be open-ended. The teacher will have hopes about what will be learned, but she must arrange things so that genuine inquiry can take place. She expects the students to make discoveries surprising to her as well as to them.

3. A variety of roles are open to the teacher, but she must eschew any role that turns her primary work into Telling; the students must be convinced that *they* will have to do the hard work of inquiry.

Readers who have never participated in such a seminar may wonder how a group of ignorant students is going to learn anything by discussing together a book that none of them understands on his own. Is this not simply the blind leading the blind? Are we not merely multiplying ignorance by bringing this "set of circumstances" into the classroom?

The Debater's Paradox

This question was raised long ago by Plato. In a dialogue called the *Meno*, Socrates seeks a definition of "virtue" in response to a question ("Can virtue be taught?") from a visitor to Athens named Meno. Socrates pursues this definition in his typical way, claiming ignorance himself, pushing Meno to define virtue, and then showing Meno the inadequacy of each definition he puts forward. The intellectual work is hard and the results frustrating, and before long Meno wants to quit. He claims that there is no way for the ignorant ever to attain knowledge, and he challenges Socrates with a series of questions:

> How will you look for it, Socrates, when you do not know at all what it is? How will you aim to search for something you do not know at all [in this case, the definition of "virtue"]? If you should meet with it, how will you know that this is the thing that you did not know?

Socrates calls this a "debater's argument." To avoid the defeatist consequences of the argument, and to convince Meno to persist with him in their inquiry into the meaning of virtue, Socrates switches tactics and proposes an unlikely metaphysical theory of the human soul. He suggests that we never really learn new things, but only "recollect" things our soul once knew (prior to birth) but has since forgotten. It is not at all clear whether Socrates believes this theory, but what *is* clear is Socrates' unwavering conviction that inquiry is worthwhile and that we should never use ignorance as an excuse to avoid its difficult demands.

Although the debater's argument presents a clever paradox (which I call "the debater's paradox"), it is rooted in a view of learning that we take for granted. If I wish to know something, my first impulse does not lead me to seek the knowledge on my own. It leads me to seek out someone who knows it and ask him to tell it to me. If I am ignorant to begin with, how else can I find the knowledge I seek?

This commonsense view grounds knowledge in the authority of other people—not just any other people, but certain special people called Authorities. This view of knowledge is promulgated by almost every culture, because it gives the culture, which has the power to designate who the Authorities are, control over what counts as knowledge. If you wish to learn what you don't know, you will naturally seek out those whom the culture designates as knowledgeable, be they priest, shaman, teacher, parent, king, or Expert.

"Some Other Process"

But this view of knowledge has a serious flaw in it, which reveals itself as soon as we ask how the Authority got *his* knowledge. We will be told, of course, that he got it from another Authority, someone he consulted when he was ignorant. But what about that Authority? We have here an infinite regress, a chain that avoids our question by constantly creating new links. There are only two possible answers to the question: Either the first link in the chain is an omniscient being whose knowledge can't be questioned (i.e., a god), or he got his knowledge from an entirely different process than being told.

Whatever his religious beliefs might have been (and he kept them to himself), Socrates had no interest in grounding knowledge of things human in the gods. And ever since the Scientific Revolution in the 17th century and the Enlightenment that grew out of it, neither have we in the West. Our culture has become secular, and with it our means for attaining knowledge. We have rejected the religious solution to the debater's paradox and so we must explore the alternative that appealed to Socrates: that knowledge is grounded in some other process than transfer from an unimpeachable Authority. If the first link in the chain acquired the knowledge in question by "some other process," then it is the *process* of attaining knowledge, and not the person who acquired it, that makes the knowledge legitimate.

We call this process "inquiry." The chief thrust of the Scientific Revolution was its development of a *kind* of inquiry that was reliable and produced spectacular results, a process that has come to be called "scientific method." Scientific method starts by doubting everything maintained by established Authorities, common sense, or cultural convention. Science could make no progress until it self-consciously wrenched itself away from the view of knowledge that had dominated human consciousness for millennia, the view built into the debater's paradox. In doing so, the scientists, mathematicians, and philosophers of the 17th century stood on the shoulders of a powerful ally from the 5th century B.C., the Socrates who swept aside the debater's paradox and insisted that Meno continue searching, relying on no authority other than *his own mind.*

"Let Us Leave Gorgias Out of It"

"His own mind"—this is the second prong of the Socratic response, which rejects the religious alternative and solves the debater's paradox by appealing to "some other process." Once we assume that the first Authority in our chain was not a god but merely a human like ourselves, and that he, therefore, attained his knowledge by "some other process," we can take the momentous step of realizing that we, too, can engage in that process which produces knowledge. At that point we can leave the first Authority in the chain, and for that matter, the entire chain, out of our consideration. If knowledge is attainable by a human process of inquiry, then we should be able to attain it for ourselves.

This conclusion is what all the Socratic dialogues point to; it is the assumption they are built on. It is the reason they are so revolutionary. And, surely, it is the reason that Socrates was put to death for corrupting the youth of Athens. For he undermined the culture's authority in the place that matters most. Over and over he insisted that we can figure out for ourselves the things that matter most without consulting cultural Authorities. He devoted his entire life to this premise, and he lived its consequences day after day, in one conversation after another. The Athenians were not wrong in sensing that he was subverting their culture.

The *Meno* opens by making just this point about individual authority. Socrates responds to Meno's question, "Can virtue be taught?" by claiming that "far from knowing whether it can be taught, I have no idea what virtue is." Meno is shocked by this confession, and asks Socrates whether he didn't hear Gorgias lecturing on virtue when Gorgias visited Athens, for Gorgias knows what virtue is, and lectures on the question most elegantly. Socrates claims not to remember whether he heard Gorgias but gets Meno to admit that he agrees with Gorgias's views on virtue. Then Socrates gives Meno the crucial stricture: "*Let us leave Gorgias out of it, since he is not here.* But Meno, by the gods, what do you yourself say that virtue is?" (emphasis added)

Socrates refuses to let Meno rely on the authority of Gorgias. His question assumes that if Meno agrees with Gorgias, it must be because Meno understands what Gorgias understood. If so, then Meno should be able to establish the meaning of virtue right now without relying on Gorgias. If he knows what virtue is, then he must have gone through the process that leads to that knowledge, and if he went through that process once in the past, he can go through it again in the present for the benefit of Socrates.

If he were able to go through that process successfully with Socrates (which he is not), then Socrates would come to understand virtue through that same process of inquiry, and his knowledge of virtue would no longer depend on Meno; he would have discovered it for himself, and the knowledge would really be his own. In conversing with others in the future, Socrates would be able to "leave Meno out of it," just as now, Meno should be able to "leave Gorgias out of it."

No longer is an appeal to Authority necessary to establish knowledge. Instead, the appeal is to a *process,* a process of inquiry that any normal adult can go through. (I shall be more explicit about this process below.) The debater's argument is false. The ignorant can proceed in good faith in their search for knowledge without relying on one who already knows.

Learning through Inquiry

And so students who meet to discuss a book they have read in common can make progress in understanding that book by inquiring together into its meaning. We have here, not the blind leading the blind, but the curious seeking to make discoveries. They will bring questions to their meeting so their search will have direction. They will select from among those questions sufficiently few so they have time to explore them in some depth. They will try to dispel their confusion by focusing on specific passages, re-reading them and paying careful attention to words, phrases, sentences, connections, connotations, implications. They will seek out contradictions in what they have said about the book and try to resolve them. They will look for matches between the experience rendered in the book and their own lives. And they will also look for mismatches. They will clutch at tentative discoveries and seek out further evidence to support them. They will also develop new questions and bring them back to their reading of the book. Everything will be submitted to joint discussion and the multiplicity of perspectives such conversation brings. Through these means, their understanding of the book will deepen.

Jessica's Journal

One of the students in Ms. Green's literature course, Jessica, keeps a journal. She loves to write and finds it natural to spend a half-hour each evening writing about her day. Here is her entry on the day Ms. Green's class started to discuss the *Iliad:*

> School was boring today except for World Lit. We started to talk about the *Iliad.* It starts out cool. Achilles loses it and almost kills his general, Agamemnon, only Athena convinces him not to. I couldn't figure out why Agamemnon was so dumb. He acted just like my kid brother. He loses his girlfriend and then takes Achilles' girl away to make up for it. Why would he piss off his best soldier?
>
> I was going to ask this question in class, but I forgot. We ended up talking about why the Greeks fought the war in the first place. It was pretty interesting. Jill and Peter got into a big fight over whether it was for honor or for booty. The rest of the class took sides and it was split pretty evenly. I didn't say anything because I couldn't make up my mind. I kept getting convinced by each person who spoke.

John gave the example of World Lit. Why would we do all the extra work that World Lit. requires when we could just take a regular English class instead? He said it was for pride, like the Greeks' honor at being the best fighters. But Mark said, "Bull." He said it was to get into college—and this was like booty. Then, Jennifer said, "Couldn't it be both?" A lot of people liked that. They said they took World Lit. for both reasons, so why couldn't the Greeks fight the war for both reasons? Most of the class agreed, but Jason insisted that each thing has only one real cause—and that there must be one cause for the war. He said the rest was rationalization. He said we might not all have the *same* reasons for taking the World Lit. course, but we each only had one *real* reason. Everyone was quiet for a minute after that. Then we started talking about Hector—and we never got back to the original topic.

Is Jason right? I took World Lit. because my parents told me it would help me get into college, but when I told my friends I was taking it, I *was* proud. And if I got accepted into college tomorrow, I wouldn't transfer out, even if I could. I hate the extra work, but I also kinda like knowing I'm doing all that work. So what *is* my real reason for taking it??? I'll have to think about this.

But wait a minute—I just realized something. Why did Agamemnon get so mad when he had to give up his girl? Was it because he hadn't seen his wife for the last nine years and really wanted some good sex with a pretty girl? Or was it because his pride was injured by having to give up *his* prize when no one else had to? *It's the same question.* Honor vs. booty. Cool! I'm definitely going to bring this up in class tomorrow.

Jessica's journal entry is not typical. She spends more words than usual on school, and she makes a discovery by reflecting on what took place in class and connecting it to her original unasked question about Agamemnon's anger. But it is not an implausible entry for a bright eighteen-year-old. It shows how a spontaneous and incomplete discussion in class can lead to significant learning.

And though the discovery recorded in the journal is still only dawning, the learning taking seed is significant. From this single entry, three distinct kinds of emerging understanding are visible: (1) Jessica is coming to *understand the story better;* she begins to see that Agamemnon's character has a childish side to it and that anger is a problematic emotion for those at war. (2) She begins to grasp a profound *general principle* about the world: Events have more than one cause. (3) She is developing an intelligent *method of reading,* connecting small questions about discrete events with big questions about the work as a whole. These are no small gains, and they have all resulted from discussing a book with others who have read it. Her teacher has told her none of these things.

The "Scientific" Spirit of the Seminar

The open-ended seminar allows the students to learn through mutual inquiry. Its method of proceeding, broadly conceived, is scientific. Its core is to *formulate hypotheses and test them against experience.*

Science may seem different because complex instruments are often required to yield the experience appealed to; in addition, complex chains of reasoning (often mathematical) may be required to connect experience and hypothesis (i.e., to generate predictions from the hypotheses). But the core of the process is the same.

Science adds the restriction that the experience appealed to in arguing for an hypothesis must be *public* and *repeatable.* We cannot accept someone's report of a private mystical experience because we have no way of knowing whether or not he is lying. The only way to ensure that he is not lying is to have the experience ourself; it must be repeatable and not exclusive to one individual consciousness.

It is also crucial to scientific method that knowledge *never* be taken as certain. The "truths" established by science are never absolute; they are always claims whose truth is a matter of less or more probability, and they are *always subject to future revision or rejection.* Precisely this spirit pervades the open-ended seminar.

Organizing the Open-Ended Seminar

In this book I am never proposing the use of one "set of circumstances" to the exclusion of all others. By recommending the open-ended seminar, I do *not* mean that a teacher should rely exclusively on this kind of class. There is a time and place for everything, and there is no reason a teacher should not tell students what she thinks they can benefit from hearing. But if she schedules *some* classes for her telling, she will find it easier to keep her mouth shut during *other* classes (such as the open-ended seminar). By refraining from telling her students what she wants them to learn by means of their seminar discussion, she preserves for them a chance of genuine inquiry.

There is no magic formula for organizing an open-ended seminar. Each teacher must find the organization that makes sense to her. In most cases, she will have to experiment considerably before settling on any one format.

Ms. Green's class on the *Iliad* represents just one moment in her quest for finding "the best way to run the seminar." For the time being, she has imposed a structured way of beginning on her students, and nothing more. The opening segment, when questions are solicited for the chalkboard, has the feeling of a ritual about it, but it also serves important educational functions.

While the chalkboard serves as a reservoir from which questions can be selected to steer the discussion, the class does not expect to go through all the questions, nor to discuss them in any particular order. But since all questions are visible on the board, they will exercise a kind of subliminal guidance on the discussion as it proceeds. Some movement from one question to another will be spontaneous, resulting from the natural flow of the discussion. At other times, a student may suggest moving on to a new question. So may the teacher.

Ms. Green sees herself as a member of the seminar group. She hopes to increase her own understanding of the *Iliad* by listening to and participating in a discussion about it. Moreover, she finds acting as a fellow inquirer an effective way to teach. She thus offers one or two questions for the board herself—questions that genuinely perplex her—but she waits until many questions are on the board before doing so, and she feels no compulsion to offer questions at every seminar.

Soliciting questions can take some time, often as much as a quarter of the whole period. It is time well-spent. First of all, it prevents the first student willing to talk from directing the conversation for an indeterminate amount of time with an ill-conceived opening comment. Second, it allows students to hear, read, digest, and even ponder a series of questions about the text before beginning to discuss any one of them. Third, it emphasizes the importance of (a) bringing questions to class, and consequentially, having thought about the reading before class, and (b) bringing *thoughtful* questions to class, questions deserving of public attention. Fourth, the ritual of writing questions on the board before discussing them creates an atmosphere of quiet intellectual deliberation in the room. It is only a slight exaggeration to call this period "the calm before the storm." Its slow pace lets students think about the book from many angles before they plunge into any one specific discussion. And it sets a tone of proper seriousness for the discussion to follow. Fifth, since there will always be questions left undiscussed by the end of class, the public list lets students take unresolved questions about the book away with them—a distinct virtue. Sixth and finally, because it is up to the students to choose the starting question, the opening ritual requires them to evaluate the *quality* of different questions. This judgment is a step in their becoming self-conscious about inquiry, since choosing where to begin involves deciding not only what is a *good* question in itself, but also what question makes a good place *to begin*.

For the class to work, one precondition must be met. Everyone must have done the reading. The point is to discuss an experience that everyone has had in common; for Ms. Green's class, that experience was reading the first three Books of the *Iliad*. Of course, to say that everyone must have read the assignment is to express an ideal; the class will still work if a few have not read it, or if a few have read some but not all of the assignment. But to the degree the ideal is not met, the class will suffer. And beyond a critical point, it simply will not work.

Included in the "everyone" who must have read the assignment is the teacher. And it does not suffice for the teacher to have read the assignment years ago, or even last year. She must read it freshly in the days preceding the class, so that the language and action of the book are fresh in her mind. She must be able to share in the experience that provides the material for discussion, and a schematic recollection from the past cannot substitute for the vivid, detailed memories that come from having recently re-read the book.

Unpredictable, Unfinished, and Surprising

The most difficult challenge for the teacher in the open-ended seminar derives from the unpredictability of spontaneous human conversation. Teachers are used to being in control. Losing control of their students may be their greatest fear. But, although a teacher can maintain civility in the seminar, she cannot engineer what is going to take place. Teachers who choose to run open-ended seminars must learn to tolerate unpredictability. If they do so, they will discover that the surprises are the biggest payoffs of the class.

As we saw from Jessica's journal entry, what happens in an open-ended seminar is not so different from what happens in an adult book group. People who have read a book in common and wish to deepen their understanding of it come together to talk about it together. They discuss selected questions, raise possible answers, examine passages from the book, bring up aspects of their personal experience that seem relevant, make connections with points raised at previous discussions.

Of course, there are *some* factors that make a student seminar quite different from a book group. First, a teacher who will grade the discussants is present in the room. Second, the students will have to produce some significant writing in essay form (on an exam, as a separate essay, or both) about the book in question, and thus they have a stronger motive for understanding the book than do the adults. Finally, they are students and they talk about books more often than typical book group members do; these conversations are a regular part of their daily life.

Nevertheless the quality of the conversation may not differ so much from what you would find at a book group of literate adults. Over time, the conversation will be desultory, electric, chaotic, focused, logically ordered, randomly ordered, pointless, fruitful. The conversation will end because time has run out, not because an ending has been reached. Typically, seminar members will leave with some questions answered to some degree of satisfaction, with others only partly answered, with others still puzzling them greatly, and with still others completely unaddressed.

From an educational point of view, this state is most desirable. It leaves them "wanting more." It leaves them thinking. It creates a suitable condition for the writing of essays. And it creates fertile ground for the continuing discussion of the *Iliad* when Books 4 – 6 are the topic of discussion, material that cannot be discussed usefully without reference to what went before.

"What went before" means not only Books 1–3, but also the seminar discussion of Books 1–3. The present discussion of Books 4 – 6 allows for bringing back to the table not only the conclusions reached in the session on Books 1–3, but also the unanswered and unaddressed questions raised in that session. The seminar builds on itself. It creates a fund of experience on which it can draw as it moves forward.

Almost anything can happen in the seminar. While there is no guarantee on any one day that anything special *will* happen, there is equally no limit to what *can* happen. A teacher must always be ready to be surprised. What may surprise her most is how much she herself learns about the book over a series of seminar discussions in which she joins her students as they struggle to come to terms with it.

What Can a Teacher Do to Help?

By setting up an open-ended seminar, the teacher offers her students a ripe opportunity for learning. But the seminar structure itself provides no guarantee that learning will take place. The teacher's work goes beyond setting up the seminar; she can improve the likelihood that learning will take place by influencing the course of the conversation.

She may act as the "seminar leader" or she may present herself as "just another member of the seminar." Either way, she need not deny that a different kind of attention will be paid to her than to anybody else. As result of both her authority and her power (see Chapter 7), a teacher is always in this position. The point is not to deny it, but to put her position of leverage to educational advantage—without turning the open-ended seminar into something else.

How can a teacher influence the course of the conversation without violating the principle that the outcome of the seminar be genuinely unpredictable? There are many ways.

One of the teacher's functions is to act as a spotlight. When she sees the group rushing past an important comment, she will focus attention on it by stopping the flow, asking the contributor to repeat the comment, and probing deeper into its implications by questioning the student further. ("What did you say, Mark? Could you say that again? Why do you think that?") In making this move, she is doing what any other class member could do, but she is also putting her knowledge and experience as a teacher to work, and she is setting an example of how to participate usefully in the conversation.

Second, she can bring in usefully posed questions to contribute to the chalkboard. Formulating fruitful questions is difficult. Students will gradually learn this skill by participating in the seminars because they will see from firsthand experience which kinds of questions stimulate useful conversations and which do not. But a teacher can speed the process along by providing good examples. Even if the students don't discuss her questions, they will notice them.

Toward the end of the opening of the *Iliad* class, Ms. Green raised her hand. When Laura called on her, she said, "The poem begins with anger. 'Anger be now your song, immortal one.' Why does the poem *begin* with anger?" This question has puzzled her for years. She feels she has only partially answered it. The question was never discussed in class that day, yet it left an imprint on Jessica without her knowing it and bore fruit in her journal entry that evening.

Third, a teacher can help the class stay focused and productive. She can help the group decide when sufficient time has been spent on one question, or when the group is spinning its wheels, and nudge them to select another question from their list. ("Why don't we look at Question #4 now?") She can point out digressions and gently steer the group back to their task. ("I've lost the connection between what we're talking about now and Brett's question. Is there one?") She can muster evidence from the book to support a hypothesis generated by a student, or in similar fashion, point to a passage in the text that undermines a proposed hypothesis. ("Listen to these lines on page 65 [she reads them]. Do they answer Jason's question?") If she is careful and retains her light touch, she can even suggest her own answers to student questions or enunciate her own dawning discoveries about the book. ("Hey! Wait a minute. Maybe *Hector* is the real hero of the poem.") In all these ways, she will simultaneously contribute to the collective inquiry and set an example of how to pursue inquiry productively.

Fourth, the teacher can help to make the conversation civil and orderly. In their enthusiasm, students often interrupt each other, ignore each other, dominate the discussion, and do many things that impede intelligent inquiry. The teacher will draw attention to these problems and ask people to change their habits in the interest of productive discussion. ("Please, guys, I can't hear what Jane is saying. Don't interrupt her. One person at a time.") But she will also try to shift the responsibility for the discussion off her own shoulders onto the group. She will periodically ask the group for its judgments on the quality of the conversation, ask for suggestions on how to make it better, and institute proposed changes in procedure if the proposals seem to her worth trying.

Fifth, at the end of a session she may summarize key results of the day's discussion so the group can hold onto what it has produced. She may alert the class to issues or questions in the next reading assignment. ("As you read the next three Books, pay attention to the change in the way the gods start behaving.") And she may discover other useful ways to bring the session to an end, to create some closure but not too much, and to point the students in the right direction for the next session.

I have not provided an exhaustive list of teacher interventions here; I have only suggested how a teacher can promote the goals of the open-ended seminar without destroying its fundamental spirit. A teacher who uses this approach regularly will discover further ways to help. She will do whatever she can to foster the learning potential of the discussion. She will listen carefully and observe closely. She will experiment and learn from her mistakes. In time, she will find many artful ways of helping the seminar flourish; in so doing she will develop her own distinctive style as a teacher of open-ended seminars.

Two Sides of One Coin

In the previous chapter, I suggested that a teacher could teach with her mouth shut by letting the books do the talking. Here I am suggesting that she may do the same thing by letting the students do the talking. In practice, these are two sides of the same coin. The chances that students will pay close attention to a great book are greatly enhanced if they have the opportunity for regular discussions of that book with peers and a restrained teacher who nonetheless knows how to make her presence felt in seminar.

A great many of the half-formed thoughts, vague intuitions, mixed feelings, and perplexities that arise in reading a book will quickly evaporate if left in their original mute state inside the student. But these same thoughts and feelings may become stable objects of attention if they are spoken aloud in a room full of people. Once publicly articulated, they have a chance to push thinking forward. A reader's immediate responses to a book are the raw materials out of which intelligent appraisal and critical interpretation are formed. They need to be captured before they disappear; they need to be made public to be further developed. The open-ended seminar is an ideal locale to make this happen.

By the same token, the seminar is not well suited for *refining* the products of textual study. Written assignments are more likely to provoke the later stages of inquiry. If essays are assigned, then this work can go on in the isolation of the writer's study, aided perhaps by informal discussion with one or two study-partners. This same kind of work will go on in response to an impending exam. Other kinds of final projects may also insure that the spontaneous, generative work of seminar gets developed to an articulate and satisfying conclusion elsewhere.

Just as the study of great books benefits from the open-ended seminar, so too does the seminar blossom when the subject under discussion *is* a great book. As I indicated above, one can have a useful seminar about any potentially educational experience. But when that experience is the reading of a great book like the *Iliad* or Toni Morrison's *Beloved,* the seminar is likely to produce more electricity. Such books invite discussion. They virtually demand mutual inquiry precisely because they pose probing questions in compelling ways and then do not answer them—or if they do suggest answers, they do not suggest obvious answers, and they do not suggest them in obvious ways. After reading such a book, one thirsts for other people to discuss it with; a seminar is just what is called for.

Under the spell of a great book, students feel the seminar to be necessary, a vital component of the reading experience itself—anything but a required ritual to satisfy a teacher. Under these conditions, a seminar is most likely to prosper. The teacher can set it up and participate in it in her own distinctive way. To whatever degree she enters into the discussion or, on the contrary, stays out of it, by creating the seminar she will be teaching well by teaching with her mouth shut.

Other Kinds of Talking

The open-ended seminar invites one kind of conversing. Students may engage in other kinds of talking as well, and to each kind corresponds a set of circumstances that the teacher may arrange to make the conversation happen. Let us briefly examine some of these other arrangements. Some are more appropriate to college than high school, but some will work equally well in both.

Formal Class Presentations

Students may speak in class by making formal presentations. Here their speech is prepared in advance and becomes the object of sustained scrutiny by the other students and the teacher. In this case, the reason for talking is not so much to stimulate inquiry as to present the fruits of one's previous inquiry.

After a formal presentation, the class will respond. Reactions can range from a small number of specific questions to a free-ranging conversation. Class discussion of whatever form continues the inquiry initiated by the presenting student. The results of his investigation are subject to public assimilation and criticism. In this way, the formal presentation becomes part of a larger cycle of inquiry.

The teacher will attend each student's presentation with interest. If she participates in the phase of response and criticism, she will do so with great care. Hers must not be considered *the* response that matters; otherwise she is on the brink of reverting to teaching-through-Telling. Before a teacher can safely try to act as a peer, she must have established a classroom culture where students really care about the response of their peers. And though the teacher must not fool herself into thinking that her remarks will weigh equally with those of everyone else, she must aspire to be an authoritative peer (whose judgment matters because of her substantial knowledge and experience) rather than the Authority whose response is the only one that matters. This may seem like a fine line, but it is a crucial one, and she must walk it. It marks the boundary between teaching with your mouth open and teaching with your mouth shut.

Out-of-Class Study Groups

There are many reasons to want students to talk to each other about their work outside of class, removed from the presence of a teacher. A teacher who assigns students to talk together and removes herself from those discussions conveys her trust in their ability to learn through mutual conversation. Once this trust is taken for granted, the odds that useful things will happen through student discussion increase dramatically.

In order to increase the chances that unmonitored student study groups will actually meet, the teacher will provide a structure for them. How much and what kind of structure will depend on the maturity of the students, the student culture of which they are part, the classroom atmosphere the teacher has created, and what happens to the "work" produced in the study groups (even if the "work" is nothing but discussion).

One teacher will assign the times and places for the groups to meet; another will prescribe the times but let the students pick the place. A third will suggest a format for the discussions. A fourth will visit occasionally. A fifth will ask students to keep journals recording the results of the discussions and to submit them for her perusal. A sixth will ask students to write evaluations of their group members' participation and take these into consideration when issuing grades.

With student study groups, no *a priori* prescriptions are called for. As always, the teacher will decide how to proceed based on her educational purposes, her knowledge of her students, and her teaching instincts. The only caveat here is that she must genuinely trust that something useful will take place when students meet and talk on their own, and this trust must be evident in her speech and behavior, as it necessarily will be if it is genuine. If she does not believe they will work, she should not be setting up study groups in the first place; she can put the students' time to better use.

Among the various kinds of study groups, each with its own proper purpose, the following three are particularly useful: (1) the "pre-seminar group," (2) the "writing group," and (3) the "pre-exam group."

The "pre-seminar group." These groups are scheduled immediately prior to each session of the open-ended seminar. They give the five to six students in each group a chance to have a first go-round at discussing the day's reading. The "pre-seminar group" allows students, first, to discuss their raw, crude reactions ("I loved it," "I hated it," "It drove me nuts") and second, to sort out basic confusions surrounding plot, character, basic concepts, and vocabulary. Such ground-clearing is essential in discussing books but can usually be dealt with effectively without a teacher's presence. These preliminary discussions preserve the time spent in seminar for the more difficult job of attacking substantive questions.

The pre-seminar group also allows students to formulate questions for the seminar, or to review, coordinate, and even synthesize questions they have already formulated. It thus promotes the presentation of more thoughtful questions to the formal seminar than would arise otherwise.

Without a teacher's presence, these groups will always have a social as well as an intellectual function. This feature is a virtue, not a vice. "Learning should be fun," we are always hearing; in the informal pre-seminar study group, it actually is. And though the amount of learning that takes place will depend entirely on the students who make up the group, even on those days when not much learning happens, other things are accomplished that increase the chance of learning in the following formal seminar.

The "writing group." This study group is designed to help students in the difficult process of writing essays. Too often teachers leave students in isolation to perform the hardest job of all: producing an articulate written essay. Forming writing groups is one way to help students with their writing. The teacher may assign one distinct activity to these groups, or may suggest several, leaving the students to decide which to adopt and when. Possible activities include: (a) generating questions to address or theses to defend in their essays, (b) reading drafts and providing reactions to the overall argument and shape of the essay, and (c) helping each other edit, correct, and polish the writing in more finished drafts.

Most students find writing difficult; nothing in school generates anxiety like the impending deadline of an essay assignment (unless it be an upcoming exam). Students are grateful for an opportunity to help each other with essay writing, and most are willing to put forth the effort needed to help others in exchange for whatever aid they might receive in return. In doing so, they learn that writing, though it must ultimately be generated in isolation, takes place most fruitfully, like the other components of inquiry, within a community.

The "pre-exam group." Nothing is more natural than the formation of student study groups in response to a forthcoming exam. In most cases, students will form groups on their own, without prodding. Who has not had the experience of getting together with some friends the night before an exam in order to study? Rather than leaving such matters to chance, the teacher need only take an extra step or two to make sure that study groups come into existence and to insure that any student who wants to can find entrance into a group.

The first step, however, is to write an exam where mutual discussion will make a difference. A vocabulary test in French may lead one student to read the list of English words aloud and another to produce the corresponding French ones on cue, but it will not lead to a discussion. Nor will any other test based on rote memorization. But any exam that poses questions requiring analysis, interpretation, or critical judgment will yield improved results as a function of prior student discussion.

One way to make study groups happen is to give out a list of questions from which the exam will be made up. Another way is to give a take-home exam, with sufficient time allotted for two stages of serious work: one in which students discuss the questions in informal groups, the other in which they write their own answers to the questions individually and separately. For a comprehensive or ambitious exam, an entire week may be appropriate. With such an exam the teacher will explicitly suggest and encourage the formation of study groups as part of "the exam process."

Under the pressure of an exam, confronting well-formulated questions, students are likely to learn more from study group discussions than under any other arrangement. The weight and nearness of the exam provide all the motivation necessary to keep students focused on the work, and the well-formulated questions provide direction and structure for the discussion. A teacher who wants students to learn from talking to each other—and who wants students to discover that they *can* learn from talking to their peers without a teacher present—can do no better than to design a challenging exam and encourage students to form study groups as a way to get ready for the exam.

In-Class Study Groups

One of the most potent ways for a teacher to keep her mouth shut in class is by using in-class student study groups. These are groups that form for one class period to work on pre-written problems or questions given them by the teacher. Since I discuss this mode of teaching at length in Chapter 6 ("Experiences That Teach: Creating Blueprints for Learning"), I will pass over it here.

Informal Out-of-Class Talking

"Informal out-of-class talking" refers to the talking students may do about their studies informally, over lunch, at the bus stop, out on a date together, as the opportunity arises. In some ways, this kind of talking is the ultimate pay-off of good teaching. If good teaching is that which yields significant learning, then good teaching will result in learning that matters to students. And what matters to students is what they will talk about with their friends. Informal out-of-class talking is an index that something useful is going on. In addition, it is a way to extend the learning that has begun in class.

Let us look in on Jennifer and Laura at the bus stop as they wait for the after-school bus to pull up at three o'clock.

Jennifer: I'm so bummed. Bill is going on a college tour during Christmas vacation and I won't see him for *ten whole days.*

Laura: Poor baby. Be glad you're not going out with Hector. Wasn't that scene with him and his wife, what's-her-name, sad?

Jennifer: Yeah, it *was* sad. But you know, it was my favorite part from what we've read so far. Hector seemed more real than any of the Greeks because he had a wife and a baby. And he wasn't so macho, you know? Sometimes it seemed as if he didn't want to fight.

Laura: I know. Do you think maybe Homer was secretly rooting for the Trojans? He makes them so sympathetic sometimes.

Jennifer: I don't know. But I'd take Hector any day over those Greek slobs. But maybe I wouldn't, really. After all, Hector gets killed, doesn't he? Anyway, what am I supposed to do for *all* of Christmas vacation? It's going to be *so* boring.

While this exchange is not profound, it shows active minds at work connecting literature with personal experience. Were I Ms. Green, I could not ask for more.

I am not suggesting any elaborate scheme here, only that teachers become aware that the formal part of what they do ought naturally to extend to the informal part of their students' lives. A teacher would do well to aspire to have her students still discussing the *Iliad* when they are waiting with their friends at the bus stop.

If her students continue to learn by discussing the *Iliad* on the bus ride home from school, they are doing so without benefit of any words from their teacher then and there. A teacher who anticipates this possibility might keep her mouth shut more during class, if only to give her students the experience of learning from each other in a setting where she still has control. Then, when she gives up her control, *which she does at the end of each school day,* she will have reason to hope they will go on with their learning—by continuing their conversation in places where they naturally get together. Teaching with your mouth shut creates ripples that spread throughout the unschooled parts of students' lives.

4

Let Us Inquire Together

Inquiry-Centered Teaching

In the previous chapter I argued that a group of students can deepen their understanding of a book in a seminar setting by inquiring together into its meaning. In this chapter I will show that pursuing inquiry together can be more than a way to describe a class activity. It can also be a way to organize an entire course. I will call such a course "inquiry-centered."

An inquiry-centered course provides the ideal setting for pursuing the kind of learning I have described in the previous two chapters. If the entire course is set up as an inquiry—the investigation of a problem or question— then reading and discussing books in an inquiring spirit will not stand out as unusual activities. They will be parts of a sustained investigation that includes *all* the course activities: reading, writing, projects, exams, reports, class discussion, classroom exercises, and whatever other means of inquiry the teacher includes.

"Why Do I Need to Learn It?"

Inquiry-centered teaching takes seriously the most plaguing question a student can put to a teacher: "Why do I need to learn it?" Most students don't voice this question, but many wish they could, and every student has the right to wonder: "Why should I devote *my* precious time to learning *your* subject?"

Algebra students who find themselves struggling with a subject that appears pointless may well ask their teacher, "Why do I need to learn algebra?" In response, the teacher might say that algebra is required by the school district and that the student needs to learn it to advance to the next grade (and eventually to graduate from high school). But should the teacher want to provide an intrinsic reason, he will have to reach. He may grope for some practical scenario to be encountered later in life where algebra will be helpful. He may praise algebra's effects on the mind or character. Or he may say that the student needs algebra so she can eventually learn calculus.

None of these reasons is convincing, and even if the student becomes persuaded in some abstract way, she probably will not become motivated to learn algebra. The connection between her present frustration and the promised benefit is too tenuous and remote to stir up any passion in her for tackling this baffling new form of mathematics. "Pie in the sky, by and by" will not do the trick.

The Great Mover

What *will* do the trick? An answer is provided by the 18th-century philosopher Jean-Jacques Rousseau: "One ought to demand nothing of children through obedience, . . . they can learn nothing of which they do not feel the real and present advantage in either pleasure or utility. . . . *Present interest—that is the great mover, the only one which leads surely and far.*" (emphasis added)

In singling out "interest," Rousseau goes right to the heart of the matter. If a student is interested in what she is learning, she will never question why she should learn it. It will not occur to her to ask why she *should* learn algebra, because she *wants* to learn algebra. But *why* does she want to learn algebra? By focusing on the word "interest," have we not simply pushed our question out of sight, rather than answered it?

Actually, we have *not* pushed the question aside. The philosopher of education John Dewey links "interest" to "need," and thereby fleshes out the concept of interest. Our interested student wants to study algebra because she *needs* algebra. She needs it *now*, not in some remote, abstract future. And why does she need it now? She needs it now in order to solve some problem with which she is preoccupied, a problem that grows organically out of her present circumstances. Perhaps she is building a radio and needs to figure out which resistors to use, what grade wire to employ, and how to set up the proper voltages. Or perhaps our student is a puzzle solver and has been given a numerical puzzle too complex to be solved by trial and error; algebra may be just what she needs to move forward and succeed.

"Why must I learn it?" may be asked about any subject. History provides a natural invitation for the question. "The past is dead and over; my concern is with the present—and the future. How is history going to be help me?"

Again, the only convincing answer will connect the required learning to the student's already existing present interest.

A student interested in fashion, for example, can be made to wonder how advertising ever came to play so dominating a role in American life. A study of that question will uncover the transformations in industry and management that took place in this country after World War I, and the huge impact on social and economic life that resulted. A student who undertakes this study will never look at fashion ads with the same eyes again.

Disequilibrium

By linking present interest to need, Dewey opens a door to a new vision of teaching. Dewey views us humans as biological organisms interacting in an environment in order to meet our needs. We use existing patterns of action— habits—to meet these needs, and life flows smoothly until we encounter some *obstacle,* thereby frustrating our attempt to reach our goal. I am used to finding my car keys in my front right-hand pants' pocket. I reach in with my right hand without thinking. My keys are gone! Where are they?? I become disturbed, frustrated, moved to find them. The encountering of an obstacle throws me off balance, creating disequilibrium.

The frustration or disequilibrium that arises from the disruption of an ongoing interaction with our world is what motivates learning. We are trying to do something and we have been stopped. We *need* to find our way around the obstacle and continue toward our goal. Suddenly we have become *interested* in solving a problem (how to get around the obstacle).

The word *interest* derives from the Latin words *inter* and *esse* ("between" and "is"). To be interested is to be between, that is, between a desire and its fulfillment. If I am keyless and need to drive my car, my interest in locating my keys will be keen.

To solve the problem, we usually need to change the way we act, modifying the habit we rely on. This is not easy, as anyone who has misplaced his keys well knows. The old habit reasserts itself—I check my pocket over and over. But the absence of keys wins the day. I am forced to look elsewhere or I remain frustrated and keyless. A new search strategy will allow me to reach my goal; the *creation* of this new strategy is what we call learning.

The pattern for mental activity is just the same. What applies to searching for keys with our hands also applies to searching for ideas with our mind. We can be just as stymied by a mental obstacle as a physical one. (See the "canary problem" on p. 16 for a puzzle that many find inherently disequilibrating, hence interesting.) An intellectual interest need not be desperate to move us. Mental needs are often less pressing than physical ones, yet they can motivate many people for weeks at a time, and some people for a lifetime.

Using Subjects Instead of Covering Them

Algebra and history teachers are not going to be helped much by the preceding discussion, however. Once Mary has solved the wiring problem for her radio, she will not return to algebra with any interest, and the lion's share of the algebra curriculum may yet lie ahead. Her problem has been solved, her need has been met, her radio is working: Why should she learn any more algebra? Similarly, once John has figured out why advertisements dominate his waking consciousness, he may ask why he should learn anything more about American history, a subject his teacher has been assigned to teach him for an entire year.

And herein lies the heart of the problem. We have used the academic disciplines (math, history, literature, etc.) as the basis for organizing our schools' curricula, and we require teachers to teach arbitrary chunks of these disciplines to students over standardized time periods. No form of organization could be more antithetical to Rousseau's insight: "Present interest—that is the great mover, the only one which leads surely and far." Most students are not interested in such abstract entities as "math" or "history"; their interests grow out of obstacles, perplexities, and blind spots that emerge from their own present, lived circumstances. By linking aspects of their subject matter to these problematic areas of experience, teachers can "create" interest in parts of "math" or "history." But rarely will they create an interest in the whole abstract subject matter (though, for the more academically inclined, certainly this can happen). And so, if they remain wedded to "math" or "history," most teachers who seek to create interest will be forced to rely on a piecemeal approach, searching out one interest for this week's work and a new one for next week's.

But an entirely different approach is possible. Rousseau's dictum invites teachers to organize their teaching around *inquiry* rather than the separate and disconnected abstractions called "history," "math," or "literature." An inquiry-centered course focuses not on traditional subject matter but on a problem or question. The subject matter is learned as a tool for working on the problem. If we wish to understand why advertising dominates our landscape, we will need to learn some social and economic history. The question "Why do I need to learn it?" is answered in advance.

Inquiry-centered courses are not labeled with the traditional subject-matter names: British Victorian Literature, American History, Micro-Economics. Their object is not to *cover* some amount of material conventionally designated by course titles. They do not aim to *cover* anything, and therefore the teacher is freed from that universal straitjacket: the demand for *coverage*—the need to get to a certain "place" by a certain date.

Instead, these courses are defined as an inquiry into a *problem* and are titled accordingly. Students learn those parts of traditional subjects they can *use* to tackle the problem, and no more. In a course called *Political Ecology* students learn large chunks of economics and biology as they wrestle with the problem of reconciling economic prosperity and environmental protection. In *Health: Individual and Community,* they master parts of biology, psychology, anthropology, and sociology in their attempt to discover whether or not there are new ways to conceive of health care.

Such a shift changes everything. To teach such a course the teacher must first have a problem—one that will interest students, and that also interests him. Once he has the problem he can then launch the investigation. It is from the investigation, the attempt to solve the problem, that learning will flow. *If the students are interested in the inquiry, then they will want to learn whatever is necessary to pursue that inquiry.* No extrinsic reasons for learning need be offered, no pie in the sky invoked.

If a student is *not* interested in the inquiry, then nothing has been gained by our shift. Teachers are not gods; they cannot create interest out of nothing. They will be wise, then, not to make any specific problem-based course a *required* course. Better to offer a choice and hope that from among an array, a student will find at least one course centered on a problem in which she is genuinely interested.

The second best avenue, one forced on a teacher who cannot sidestep his institution's requirement that students take his course, is to try to *awaken* some interest in the inquiry. This is not always possible but also not as hard as it sounds. If the teacher keeps one eye on the nature of the student population and another on the spirit of the times, he can usually forge a connection between actual student interests and the problem that defines the inquiry. It is far easier to create an interest in a problem-centered inquiry than it is to create one in "algebra" or "American History."

Killing Two Birds with One Stone

In 1991, facing a hole in my projected teaching schedule for 1993, I had the opportunity to develop a new course. Ever since I first encountered him in a freshman philosophy course, I had always been fascinated by the figure of Socrates. Over the years, I had read most of the early dialogues of Plato (the so-called "Socratic" dialogues). As a teacher, I had taken inspiration from Socrates, but like most readers of these texts, I was far from thinking that I understood this enigmatic character. I wanted to learn more about Socrates, to think more about him, and I also thought that students would find an intensive study of the Socratic texts exciting and valuable. So I decided to design an inquiry-centered course on Socrates, "killing two birds with one stone," which inquiry-centered teaching always does. I called the course *In Search of Socrates*.

Searching for Socrates

> As Socrates says in Plato's *Apology*, "The unexamined life is not worth living." Who knows? Maybe it is. But, I will tell you something, it is worth exploring and contemplating whether or not the examined life is more preferred. We will never know if the unexamined life is not worth living until we examine it. (from a student's reflection on her work in *In Search of Socrates* [*ISOS*])

In Search of Socrates was inquiry-centered because it was organized around a question. The question that organized it was the one that moved me to teach it in the first place. Though at heart a single problem, it is best put as a series of overlapping questions: Who was Socrates? What was he trying to do? Why did he carry on philosophical conversations in the frustrating manner depicted in the dialogues? Why does no one apparently ever learn anything from these conversations? Why did Socrates live his life the way he did? Why did he die the way he did? Was he a great teacher, as history has taken him to be? Or was he no teacher at all, as he, himself, repeatedly insisted? The figure of Socrates as painted by Plato is one large paradox. I wanted to get students to confront this paradox and form a group inquiry around it.

What is wonderful about this particular inquiry is that scholars and intelligent readers have been struggling with these questions for over 2000 years. I could honestly say to my students that they had just as much chance as anyone to crack the puzzle. "Great scholars have spent lifetimes tackling it and failed," I told my students. "It may well be that a fresh and naive approach will yield better results." These words do not offer a false promise to students; they may well be true! It would certainly help to know ancient Greek and be able to read the texts in the original, but a knowledge of Greek has not led anyone to solve the problem successfully. The translations available are excellent. And studies written by scholars who do know Greek are available in the library in any number desired.

Unlike many problems that may organize classroom inquiry, this one has no intrinsic interest for someone who has not read about or heard of Socrates. But Plato's early dialogues are so engaging and puzzling that it takes no more than reading one of them (and they are short) for the questions that define this inquiry to jump to life and grab hold of the students. Thus, students who signed up for the course named *In Search of Socrates* had their own idiosyncratic reasons for doing so, but after the first reading assignment, they suddenly found themselves joined together in a common quest.

> One of the most amazing things about this class is how the material gets under your skin. You begin by examining the nature of day-to-day things, the mundane, and end by questioning yourself and the meaning of life itself. As Nicias states in *The Laches:* "[A]nyone who is close to Socrates and enters into conversation with him is liable to be drawn into an argument, and whatever subject he may start, he will be continually carried round and round by him, until at last he finds that he has to give an account of both his present and past life, and when he is once entangled, Socrates will not let him go until he has completely and thoroughly sifted him (187e–188b)." (from another student's reflection on her work in *ISOS*)

Searching for Socrates Together

While inquiry can be carried on in isolation, in most cases combining the powers and perspectives of many minds yields better results. Thus, the pursuit of knowledge is usually conducted within scientific and intellectual communities. Thinkers convey the results of their research to each other; they build on each other's work; and they rely on each other's criticism.

Inquiry-centered teaching becomes more powerful when it emphasizes *group inquiry*. Despite the requirement that each student eventually develop her own interpretation of Socrates, *In Search of Socrates* was a group endeavor through-and-through.

> With Plato's dialogues I could not simply read the text once, and then understand everything that he intended to get across to the reader. Only by reading the dialogues two or even three times was I able to pick out what seemed to be Socrates telling the interlocutor (or even the reader) how to live one's life. But then my interpretation would at times be refuted in seminar by someone who had the opposite interpretation. This forced me to not only assess my own interpretation, but up to 22 others. So I'd sit back in seminar, or at home, and converse with myself, or others, debating which opinion or interpretation was the best, wondering at times what was the connection between the logic in the dialogues and the meaning of virtue. This was how I learned to compare and basically intertwine my interpretations with everyone else's, for [neither] my nor anyone else's interpretations [ever] seemed totally incorrect or correct. (another *ISOS* student)

The group included the students *and* their teacher. If I was to stimulate genuine group inquiry, there had to be a place in the overall investigation for me, too. My inquiry was not at the same level as those of my students; I had a head start on them. But it was about the same question.

My students and I never pretended to be equal in knowledge or experience by virtue of our common membership in this group. Scientific communities almost always consist of unequals as well as equals (think of lab assistants and graduate students, both vital contributors to scientific research). But by sharing a curiosity in the same problem and a commitment to work together on that problem, we came together as members of a common intellectual community.

The shift to inquiry-centered teaching changes most aspects of classroom life and allows the teacher to teach with his mouth shut. It is the inquiry that teaches. The inquiry teaches because the process of inquiring induces one to learn. I expected to learn from the course I had set in motion, just as my students did. And we expected to share the results of our learning with each other.

> Other students had such radically different opinions than my own that I was often compelled to reconsider my positions (I did at least three major flip-flops in my thinking on Socrates over the quarter). I think I contributed a great deal to seminar and gave a point of view that no one else came close to expressing. The fact that I was cited in several of my classmates' papers makes me think I contributed valuably. Seminar drove home Socrates' point that learning must be a group activity. (another *ISOS* student)

The Inquiry Dictates the Course Design

Making up the reading list for *In Search of Socrates* was not difficult. The problem that defined the inquiry also suggested what we needed to read to conduct the investigation. We read most of Plato's early dialogues, as many as time allowed. (There are about 14.) We read them at a fairly leisurely pace, and since re-reading is essential with these materials, time for re-reading was built into the syllabus. I also made sure the students had ample time to discuss these dialogues with each other, for these are texts that demand discussion.

Plato dominated the reading list, but there were other authors, too. Most important were the two other contemporaries of Socrates who wrote about him and whose works survive—Xenophon and the comic playwright Aristophanes. These two authors provide perspectives on Socrates very different from Plato's and help students gain at least some distance from Plato's compelling point of view. Finally, it proved useful to expose students to a few interpretations of Socrates by later scholars and critics. I wanted to show them what a coherent interpretation of Socrates looks like and how one goes about defending it. I also invited three colleagues, each with his own pointed view of Socrates, to lecture to the class.

I, myself, never once lectured. I feared that doing so would kill or dampen the ethos of mutual inquiry that was vital to the course. Instead, I occasionally leapt to my feet during seminar discussions for quick impromptu talks, filling in necessary historical information, or information about the Greek equivalents of key philosophical terms used repeatedly in the dialogues. I kept these talks brief (four or five minutes) and gave far fewer of them than you would imagine. And I only presented information that bore on what was being discussed at the time.

The Teacher's Work

I taught this course with my mouth shut. I relied on the inquiry itself to do the teaching. That meant "letting the books do the talking" and, just as much, it meant "letting the students do the talking." But it left me with plenty to do. Aside from popping up with my tidbits of information (the least of my teaching activities), I had five major jobs: (1) I had to *organize* the inquiry for my students; (2) I had to figure out how to use my own analysis of the materials to *help the students understand* the texts—without imposing my understanding on them and thus robbing them of the inquiry that defined the course of study; (3) I had to *help my students develop the skills* necessary to pursue the inquiry; (4) I had to *evaluate* each student's work so I could give grades at the end of the course, and, lest we forget my initial motive, (5) I had to *participate* in the inquiry myself.

Organizing the Inquiry

In any but the most advanced inquiry-centered course, organizing the inquiry remains the teacher's primary task.

Reading.   First, I had to select the books. I have already mentioned the books from which I made my reading assignments. I was not explicit about my reading list because the number of readings chosen will depend on the amount of time at the teacher's disposal. But book *selection* is only the first step in making up the syllabus. Book *sequencing* is almost as important. Since none of Plato's early dialogues can be dated, either absolutely or even relatively with respect to each other, ordering by chronology was not possible. I decided to start with the simplest dialogues and work up to the more complex, with some exceptions.

I inserted the "biographical" dialogues early in the sequence, but not at the very start, and I saved one or two "quirky" dialogues for the end, to be used as "test cases" after the progression from simple to complex was completed.

Most important, I made the question of sequencing part of the inquiry itself. Late in the course I provided an exercise in which students had to contemplate two alternative sequences of the very works they had read alongside the order they had actually followed. I asked them to discuss what difference each ordering would have made on the conclusions they were drawing about Socrates. ("Large differences," they decided.) This simple exercise helped offset the inevitable biasing that the selected order created in their thinking (as any order must), and also helped them become self-conscious about the process of inquiry itself.

Class activities. The next step in organizing the inquiry required mapping out the class activities for each week. I met the class four days a week, twice early in the week, and twice late in the week. Each two-day cluster was used to examine one reading assignment. One of the two days was an "open-ended seminar" on the work (see Chapter 3); the other was a teacher-directed class, usually a "conceptual workshop" (see Chapter 6). None of these teacher-directed classes were lectures, and in none of them did I "explain what a text meant" or present my own understanding of Socrates directly. However, I used my evolving understanding to organize discussions of various kinds, and students were well aware that I was doing so. They got to try out and test my ideas about the texts without having them imposed on their own thinking. In some of these exercises, I presented alternative interpretations of the same text; in others I had them assess particular arguments within a dialogue; in still others I focused on themes or concepts that play a major role across many dialogues. (See p. 98 for an example of one of these exercises.)

I thus led my students to examine concepts that I deemed central, prodded them to make connections among different works, and asked them to try to gradually synthesize the accumulating body of "evidence" about Socrates as it built. Because I, myself, was engaged in the inquiry, I had no monolithic interpretation to impose; my own interpretations tended to be local and tentative, and my view of Socrates shifted from dialogue to dialogue. As a consequence, I felt confident that my teacher-directed classes would not subtly impose a uniform interpretation (my own) on the students, and their final papers proved me right. On the other hand, I recognize that my views inevitably had *some* effect on their thinking.

In addition, students were required to form "pre-seminar study groups" (see Chapter 3) and to meet in these groups without me for an initial discussion of the day's readings prior to each of the week's two seminars. These sessions, in addition to enhancing the seminar discussions for the reasons discussed in Chapter 3, strengthened the spirit of inquiry throughout the course. They demonstrated to the students my faith in their ability to learn something significant through mutual discussion and examination of the texts on their own.

Writing. The final step in organizing the course inquiry was to plan and sequence the students' writing assignments. Students engaged in inquiry have to write regularly. Only by transforming their tenuous, emergent thinking into hard, clear words on paper will they be able to see what they think as they are thinking it. And only by writing will they be able to push their thought as far as they can. Finally, writing is required for the best communication of their thinking to each other. Without written products, the mutual aspect of the group inquiry is limited to the fleeting and often disorganized speech of spontaneous discussions. When students are asked to read each other's papers and provide written critique in response, they take the time necessary to consider the thinking of their peers carefully and seriously. Their own thinking is sharpened as a result.

So organizing the writing in the course had two dimensions to it. The first was to devise a structure so that students not only could, but would, read and respond to each other's essays. This structure is described in Chapter 5. In brief, students had to submit the essays they wrote every other week into a Class Notebook made available on the reserve shelf of the library. On alternate weeks, when no essays were due, they had to write response letters to two papers of their own choosing in the notebook. This system got the students to read each other's essays, and they found they appreciated reading each other's work more than they anticipated, since the more ideas they were exposed to in their own searches for Socrates, the happier they were. It also got them to take the entire class as their audience when writing, rather than just a single teacher.

The second dimension was to formulate the writing assignments themselves. *In Search of Socrates* lasted ten weeks. I wanted my students writing every week, but I wanted them writing both formal essays *and* informal response letters. So I assigned five formal essays. The essay assignments, like virtually everything else in the course, were dictated by the aim of the inquiry. The final essay had to address the question at the center of the program inquiry: What was the point of Socrates' life? The remaining essays had to get the students ready to write the final one.

For the fourth essay, I asked for a critical evaluation of someone else's interpretation of Socrates. I figured this would help them crystallize their emerging view of Socrates without forcing it to premature closure. Each of the first three essays was a focused inquiry into one dialogue, an attempt to answer a question posed by the student herself about the dialogue. These essays were necessary to stimulate close reading, careful analysis, and reasoned argument, the foundations on which their wider interpretation of Socrates would have to rest.

Cumulative inquiry. From the student's point of view, the inquiry consisted of a repeating pattern of weekly activities—reading, pre-seminar study groups, two kinds of formal classes, one or another kind of writing, more reading, and so forth. But beneath these activities lay the experience of a cumulative inquiry, where each experience built on the one before it.

> Realizing I didn't know anything wasn't a one-time-only, get-it-while-you-can lesson. Every night Plato's puzzling text exchanged hours of concentrated reading for questions, questions, questions. What distinguished Socrates from the Sophists? Why was he killed? Is knowledge possible? (another *ISOS* student)

Over the ten weeks the students started thinking about Socrates and they never stopped thinking about him. They formed their initial ideas based on their initial readings, and they modified those ideas based on other people's understanding of those same readings as they heard it expressed in class discussion and as they read it in other students' papers. They modified their ideas further as they read new dialogues by Plato, and still further as they read Xenophon's account of Socrates. They developed new ideas, gave them up, went back to old ideas previously rejected, combined ideas, threw their hands up in despair, started all over again, moaned with each other about how impossible the inquiry was, bragged to students outside the class about how important the inquiry was, and just kept at it. At times, some, like Meno, were tempted to quit, but their fellow students wouldn't let them. (And after they had read the *Meno*, they were too ashamed to quit!) In the tenth week, they had the joy of finishing for now what they knew could never be finished—their account of Socrates, of reading each other's tentative final conclusions, and of having their own made public.

> How should you live your life? What do you believe? In the course *In Search of Socrates* these are the questions we dealt with every day. In our search for a man whose life ended over 2000 years ago we found the questions he raised still important to us today. Our search led straight to the heart of all of us as we faced these questions ourselves. For the search for Socrates became a search for myself. The course raised many questions for me and started me thinking more seriously about my future. (another *ISOS* student)

Helping Students Understand

My second job, putting my own thinking at the students' disposal, I did by means of classroom exercises called "conceptual workshops." I have alluded to these in passing (without naming them) in Chapter 3 under the heading of "in-class study groups." Since I will discuss this form of teaching at length in Chapter 6, I will pass over it now.

Helping Students Develop Skills

My third job, helping students develop the skills necessary to pursue the inquiry, is not entirely distinct from the second. I separate them because I want to distinguish between the development of *understanding* and the development of *skills*. But in practice they are not so easy to distinguish, and in this course, the conceptual workshops promoted the development of both at the same time (e.g., the skill of analysis and an understanding of the text).

But in some instances, the distinction is clear-cut. If students need to rely on the library as part of their inquiry, they may need to learn some tactics for using a library effectively. If they need to use a lab, they will need to learn lab techniques. In this particular course, they needed to learn the following skills:

1. to analyze logical arguments
2. to analyze dramatic action
3. to detect irony
4. to formulate useful questions about complex texts
5. to write expository essays addressing a clear question and defending a thesis in response to that question
6. to constructively criticize the essay writing of their peers
7. to converse constructively, critically, and civilly with fellow students about complex, provocative texts.

I worked hard to help my students develop each of these skills, but I did not separate the teaching of these skills into separate "units," divorcing this learning from the inquiry itself. Instead, I addressed the skills *in situ,* as they were needed in the students' pursuit of the inquiry. I did not say, "First learn to write, then write about Plato," but rather, "Learn to write by writing about Plato." In life, form and content are never separate, and in learning they are usually best confronted together. There is no better way to learn to analyze arguments or to detect irony than to examine Plato's arguments or Plato's irony. There is no need to "get ready" first. Practicing these skills on vapid content eradicates interest in learning; it leads instantly to the question: "Why do I need to learn it?"

In thinking about skills, we can clearly see how an inquiry-centered course satisfies the standard objectives of teaching, even though it doesn't take them on as its foremost aims. We can see here the power of Dewey's approach. The students will engage in mastering academic skills precisely because they see and feel how necessary these skills are as tools in the pursuit of their inquiry. And they are already interested in the inquiry; they have developed a *need* to understand Socrates! My students never asked me why they needed to learn to analyze logical arguments; they were already struggling to do so simply to make sense of Socrates' refutations of Meno's definitions of virtue.

Evaluating Students' Work

My fourth job, evaluation, was straightforward enough. I evaluated each student essay in the traditional manner, for clarity, coherence, intelligence, the strength of its argument, and how interesting it was. Each student's final grade derived primarily from her written work, with "class participation" adding only a small amount on top.

There is nothing new here about evaluation, but the topic bears mentioning for three reasons. First, reading and evaluating regular essays by a classroom full of students is a demanding and time-consuming job. A teacher who takes it seriously will find it takes more of his teaching time than any other single activity. It is worth mentioning if only to dispel any notion that "teaching with your mouth shut" results in any less work on the part of a teacher who adopts this posture.

Second, evaluating essays is a form of teaching in itself. Evaluation may be necessary to produce a grade at the end of the course, but its more important justification is that *students can learn from being evaluated.* They can learn to identify their strengths and weaknesses in both thinking and writing, and they can learn what to do about their weaknesses in order to improve.

Third, I would point out that I have spoken of grades in this example only to keep things simple. In the college where I teach (The Evergreen State College), grades are never given; they are replaced by written narrative evaluations that become part of the student's formal transcript. Teachers write brief essays that describe students' strengths and weaknesses, and their specific accomplishments in the particular course; they are not forced to average or collapse all those details into one letter grade. The absence of grades at the college encourages the spirit of collaboration necessary for group inquiry. That is why I mention it here. A teacher whose institution allows him to dispense with letter grading would do well to do so in pursuing an inquiry-centered course. But one without that option need not despair. As long as he keeps grades in the background and organizes his course so that *competition for grades* is kept to a minimum, a teacher should have no trouble fostering group inquiry in his classroom.

Participating in the Inquiry

Finally, my fifth job delighted me the most. It was my reason for teaching *In Search of Socrates* in the first place. I had to participate in the inquiry myself. This demand is not just "frosting on the cake"; it goes to the heart of this approach to teaching. If I say to my students, "Let us inquire together," I had better mean it. There is no faking genuine involvement in an inquiry, and if a teacher tries to fake it, he will be found out by his students at once. "Why don't all of you have an inquiry? I'll watch, and also help you," might work better than Telling, but it doesn't compare with "Let us inquire together." And so I deepened my own understanding of Socratic philosophy by means of the inquiry I used to teach Socrates to my students.

I read new works on Socrates while my students were reading ones I knew well. I re-read familiar works with new eyes. I noticed new aspects. I pushed my own thinking. Class discussion provoked new thoughts in me. So did the students' papers. In seminar, the students saw that I was as engaged as they were. I brought my own questions to class. I listened carefully. If I made a discovery in class, I sometimes blurted it out with excitement. I participated fully in the intellectual community that *was* the course.

> I think Don's greatest benefit to the course was his enthusiasm and interest in the course material. He demonstrated this interest by taking part in Seminar as an equal participant [and by] reading massive amounts of literature to prepare the workshops. . . . Don offered his own beliefs during or after the group's discussions and his views were presented as possible solutions just as if he was another student in the course. (from an *ISOS* student's evaluation of me)

This participation was my reward for teaching with my mouth shut by inviting students to inquire with me. It was also the secret engine that made my classroom hum with excitement. Intellectual excitement is contagious; a teacher can infect his students with a passion for inquiry without their even noticing.

> This quarter has been both confronting and exhilarating. The search for Socrates demanded an examination of my deepest beliefs. Socrates' true identity continues to elude me, much the way a definition of virtue escaped

him. As a result, I have grown to appreciate the search, and value the striving as much as the goal. (another *ISOS* student)

Interdisciplinary Teaching

Problem-centered teaching is naturally interdisciplinary because the focus is on a question, and most interesting questions can be usefully examined from the perspectives of several disciplines.

But the polarity "interdisciplinary vs. disciplinary" does not automatically translate into "broad vs. narrow," as one might imagine. The inquiry that fueled *In Search of Socrates* was highly focused, centering on one quasi-historical/quasi-fictional character—Socrates. Narrow as it was, the inquiry was interdisciplinary. Plato, though considered the West's most influential philosopher, wrote at a time before the differentiation between philosophy and literature had become complete. His philosophical works take literary form; each is a play (perhaps they were even performed). If you approach them either as purely philosophical or as purely literary works, you do a grave injustice to the texts, ignoring half of what is present on the page.

In this course, my students and I didn't worry about disciplinary boundaries; we tried to investigate each text on its own terms, taking into account as much of what was on the page as we could. We used tools from both literary and philosophical disciplines, but we didn't label them or worry about what subjects we were studying at any given moment. We were too busy trying to figure out what Socrates was up to.

One could just as easily design a purely disciplinary inquiry that is widely construed. As an example, I recently taught a literature course on Shakespeare and Chaucer that explored what it means to consider these two great writers as "educators" and why the study of literature is considered an important component of a good education.

While *In Search of Socrates* was interdisciplinary, I was able to teach it alone because I have training and experience in both literature and philosophy. Many teachers have sufficiently broad interests and background to teach interdisciplinary courses on their own. For those who don't, team teaching provides the most natural way to mount an interdisciplinary course. An interdisciplinary course that focuses on health creates a natural setting for a biologist and a social scientist to team up. Courses such as American or Japanese Studies invite a historian and a literature teacher to join forces. Environmental Studies typically brings together a natural scientist and a social scientist.

Inquiry-centered courses, because they focus on problems rather than fields, naturally invite team teaching. They do so because so many interesting problems bridge separate disciplines. Not all schools make room for team-taught courses, but many do, even though they treat them as special cases.

Where interdisciplinary teaching is a possibility, inquiry-centered teaching becomes a natural way to realize its potential.

The topic of team teaching, especially a particular species of team teaching termed "collegial teaching," opens up a whole new set of questions. These questions are germane to the theme of this book, and collegial teaching is one of the most dramatic and unusual ways to teach with your mouth shut. This topic is too broad to be treated in this chapter; I will discuss it in a chapter of its own (Chapter 8).

A Variety of Inquiries

I have discussed *In Search of Socrates* at length in order to flesh out how a course can be organized around inquiry instead of coverage. To give a sense of the variety of possible questions that can usefully serve as the basis of inquiry-centered teaching, I include the following list of courses taught at Evergreen at one time or another, each of which I taught as either the sole teacher or a member of an interdisciplinary faculty team. I leave it to the reader's imagination to picture what these courses might have looked like or felt like. For each, I list the course title, the question or problem that organized the inquiry, the traditional fields of study included, and the number of teachers.

1. *"Polis" and Psyche: Greece, Europe, and the United States.* How are the psychological dimension of human experience and the political dimension of human experience related to each other? More specifically, what are the implications of what we know about human psychology for the human capacity for self-government? Fields of study: political philosophy, psychology of personality, and literature. One teacher.

2. *Great Stories.* What is the effect of the physical or symbolic medium in which a story is told (e.g., speech, writing, film) on the story's meaning and the story's impact? (In this course, science and math were considered to be concerned with telling stories.) Fields of study: literature, philosophy, and history of science and mathematics. Five teachers.

3. *Meaning, Learning, and Power: Constructing an Education.* How are "meaning," "learning," and "power" best understood? How is each of these three concepts related to the other two? How might our understanding of them inform our aims and means in education? Fields of study: philosophy, psychology, and social science. Three teachers.

4. *States of Nature.* What is the effect of our conception of "nature" on our views of human happiness, human freedom, and human development? And how have conceptions of nature in the West changed historically? Fields of study: literature, philosophy, and history of science and mathematics. Four teachers.

5. *Development: The Aim of Education.* What are the consequences for teaching that come from taking "development" to be the aim of education? Fields of study: philosophy of education, developmental psychology, and social psychology. One teacher.

Making Learning Personal

Because inquiry-centered courses are organized around a problem that students become *interested* in, they inevitably become personal. If a teacher succeeds in turning his classroom into a genuine intellectual community, if the energy that drives the course flows from the students' real *need* to investigate the question they hold in common, then the learning that results can touch students deeply. I believe this to be true in any course centered on inquiry, but with Socrates at the center of the inquiry, it was inevitable. Here are several more students from *In Search of Socrates* commenting on the course's impact on them.

> *In Search of Socrates* not only taught me about Socrates and philosophy but, even more importantly, I learned that in the right environment, education has no limits. It has helped me discover an inner voice I never knew I had. This voice has awakened inquiry within me and its presence urges me on.

> On a different level, the greatest gift this class has given me is that it has reinvigorated my drive to learn. It has filled me with questions rather than tried to fill me with answers, which is what I think Socrates tried to do to his interlocutors. Although I am exhausted, I am also excited to continue my search for self-understanding and the meaning of my education. Socrates has leaked into my life like water and is affecting every nook and cranny of who I am. The dialogues have forced me to examine my entire life and this examination has broken down convictions I once held, leaving empty spaces. Emptiness is not necessarily painful and I am looking forward to taking some time off from school next year, getting used to the spaces left inside me.

> Through my association with Socrates I've learned that I am a rhetorician. I am not proud to say that, after following Socrates around the agora and participating in this community of inquiry. But prior to this course, if someone had asked me what do you know how to do, I would have said—persuade people. Now, fresh from the Socratic sifter, I believe this way of life, that of rhetoric, to be dangerous to one's soul—dangerous to my soul.

> This course has honestly changed my life. The course forced me to question almost everything about myself, and I'm still searching for some of the an-

swers. The question of how a man should live his life is so perfectly articulated in Plato's writing that it is impossible for me to ignore it. I must try my best to answer it. . . . [*In Search of Socrates*] wasn't so much a college course as it was a ten week lifestyle alteration. It was an amazing experience of self discovery and philosophical learning. This course has crystallized the question of how I should live my life; now I need to answer that question—a life's work.

Let Us Inquire Together

By presenting my students with the serious invitation, "Let us inquire together," I offered them a fresh and invigorating opportunity to learn. By creating *In Search of Socrates,* I offered to teach them with my mouth shut.

Because I organized the course as an inquiry, I freed myself from the restricting restraints of coverage. I did not have to teach Philosophy 101 or Early Plato. The course title implied a question, not an amount of territory, and I taught the course as a means to pursue the question. With a good question like this one, I could never run out of pertinent material; there was thus no hope of ever "covering" it all. All I could do was to examine enough material to stimulate a good inquiry. But the point of "examining material" had now shifted. It was not to attain familiarity with it or knowledge of it; it was to *use* it to attack an interesting problem.

My job was defined by the spirit of inquiry in general and the nature of the specific inquiry I had selected. I based my choices on what would engender the best inquiry, and, in making those choices, I had to take into account the nature of my students.

Both during and after *In Search of Socrates,* my students raved to their friends and parents. They didn't rave about me, their teacher; they raved about the course! They raved about Socrates, about Plato, about each other, about *what they were doing together.* If asked specifically about their teacher, they had words of praise to offer, but their attention was not riveted on me. By keeping my mouth shut and organizing an engaging inquiry, I had allowed them to focus their attention on subjects that deserve attention: on Socrates, on Plato, on the moral questions Socrates posed to his fellow citizens, and on the process of inquiry itself. Students who tend to forget about their teacher in their enthusiasm over Socrates and in their struggle to come to terms with Socrates are far different from those dazzled students (in Chapter 1) who left the lecture hall wanting to be like their godlike teacher but knowing they never could be. These students already *are* like their teacher, but in focusing on Socrates they never think to compare themselves with him.

5

—

Speaking with Your Mouth Shut
The Art of Writing

In the last three chapters, I have argued that an important part of the art of teaching lies in organizing an engaging inquiry for students. Essay writing is indispensable to student inquiry; the previous chapter showed its pivotal function in one inquiry-centered course. In this chapter, I shall address writing directly, both the students' and the teacher's.

In Part II of this chapter, I will discuss an organization that puts student writing at the center of the intellectual experience of a course: the writing community. But first, in Part I, let us see how a *teacher's* writing can become a powerful teaching tool. It is possible to "teach through writing" and still keep your mouth shut.

Part I: Teaching Through Writing

The Paradox of the Phaedrus

I have long been fascinated by a paradox that surfaces in one of Plato's dialogues, the *Phaedrus*. At the end of the dialogue, Plato provides a pointed critique of the relatively new technology of his age: writing. Writing, Plato argues, ruins the capacity for memory. Worse, it substitutes only the appearance of wisdom for wisdom itself. Socrates tells Phaedrus the story of a king who rejects the gift of writing offered to him by a god with these words:

> And it is no true wisdom that you offer your disciples, but only its semblance, for by *telling* them of many things without *teaching* them you make them seem to know much, while for the most part they know nothing, and

as men filled not with wisdom, but with the conceit of wisdom, they will be a burden to their fellows. (emphasis added)

Writing cannot teach, says Plato. Reading cannot lead to knowledge. At best, a written text serves merely as a reminder of what the reader already knows.

> Then anyone who leaves behind him a written manual, and likewise anyone who takes it over from him, on the supposition that such writing will provide something reliable and permanent must be exceedingly simpleminded ... if he imagines that written words can do anything more than remind one who knows that which the writing is concerned with.

Finally, Plato levels the charge against writing that it cannot be questioned. If questioned, a written document maintains "a majestic silence," and though it may seem intelligent, it just "drifts all over the place, getting into the hands not only of those who understand it, but equally of those who have no business with it."

In the context of the whole dialogue, this critique implies that spoken conversation of the Socratic kind is the form of discourse proper to the cultivation of wisdom and knowledge and that writing is not only inferior, but is downright destructive because it fosters the *illusion* of knowledge.

Readers who admire this critique nevertheless can't help noticing that it comes to them in the form of a written text. If Plato held the opinion of writing that he puts in Socrates' mouth in this dialogue, why then did he write? Why didn't he follow the lead of the teacher who made such a mark on him and restrict his philosophizing to spoken conversation, as Socrates himself did?

History provides no answer to this question; we know little about Plato's life. So we are left with a paradox—a written text that condemns writing—and we are left to our own devices in confronting it.

My own response to this paradox is to hypothesize that Plato did not write for a general, anonymous public. After Plato decided to give up on politics, a career toward which his aristocratic birth naturally pointed him, he founded the first university in the West: the Academy (the source of our words *academy* and *academic*). I like to think of Plato's writings as "learning exercises" designed for his students in the Academy—and only for them. This would explain both why they take the form of dialogues and why, in so many of them, no philosophical conclusions are ever reached by the participants. With the shorter dialogues at least, I imagine Plato using his written texts just to get the conversation started, expecting his students to take up in living speech the conversation from the point where it broke off on the page.

I shall not try to convince you that this was Plato's purpose in writing; I cannot even convince myself. Rather, by conjuring up this possibility, I want to suggest an unusual way in which writing can be used as a vehicle for teaching. Whether Plato did so or not, a teacher can speak to her students through writing, thereby keeping her mouth shut while still addressing them in words.

Direct vs. Indirect Speech

When a teacher lectures or expounds to students, she talks *directly* to them. The same is true when a teacher speaks one-on-one to a student in her office or informally in the hallway. But if a teacher were to write to a student, say a letter, she would be speaking *indirectly* to the student. Even though she might express the same content in speech as on the page, the latter is indirect because the teacher is not physically present when the message is delivered. The message does not come to the student through the "hot" medium of the teacher's spoken voice, but through the "cool" medium of words written on the page.

The student listening to his teacher's spoken words must listen at the speed at which the teacher speaks, must hear all her tones and inflections of speech, see her facial gestures and body language; for better or worse (for better *and* worse), he falls under the spell of his teacher's personality.

But the student reading his teacher's written words can read at his own pace, pause and think, re-read certain passages or the whole piece; he is spared the embodied tonal and gestural imperatives that accompany spoken language. Some distance has opened up between himself and his teacher, and he reads her words in the relative calm of that space that now separates them. His teacher's personality will still affect him, but not so directly, not so immediately, not with so much power. As a result of getting to *read* his teacher's words (1) the student will be more likely to digest those words and, (2) he will be more likely to formulate a response to them.

Let us examine three disparate ways of "teaching through writing." Each is a way to teach with your mouth shut by writing to students.

"Dear Anna, I read your essay with particular interest because . . .": Teacher Response Letters

Anyone who has ever been a student remembers the experience of getting an essay returned marked up with red ink. First, you found the grade, then you turned to the last page to check out the two or three sentences—or perhaps it was just a phrase—in which your teacher summarized her reaction to your paper. If you were conscientious, you studied the corrections and commentary in red ink that ran through the paper but usually not until later.

As a student I was one of the conscientious ones, and I learned how to improve my writing by studying my teacher's brief comments and many corrections. And so, when I began to teach, I responded to my own students' essays in the traditional manner. After quite a few years, it dawned on me that my students were not as conscientious as I had been. There was little evidence that they were reading, much less scrutinizing, my editorial and critical markings, and their writing didn't improve visibly with each successive paper.

Gradually, over much more time than I care to admit, I evolved a different means of evaluating and responding critically to my students' essays. Now I write a personal letter to each student. The letter begins, "Dear So-and-so," and it ends, "Sincerely, Don." I staple it to the front of the essay and hand the whole thing back as one packet.

In these letters I address what seems most important to me about the essay: My subjects range from the most substantive to the most technical, from the paper's main idea to its misuse of commas. I try to limit myself to two or three points in each letter. I choose these points by asking myself: "If I were the author of this paper, what reactions of a reader would help me most?" I do, however, always try to include points of strength as well as points of weakness, and I almost always begin by writing about the strengths. I include strengths not to "candy coat the medicine," but because I believe that writers can learn as much from becoming aware of what is strong in their writing as from detecting its flaws. I *begin* with strengths because people who get to hear what you honestly find strong in their writing are more willing to listen to your report of where the writing suffered.

I write personally and with feeling, sometimes with humor, and I always try to pitch my writing to the individual student. Because I write quickly, my letters are fairly long. Before I start my letter, I always retrieve from my computer files my previous letter to that student to remind myself of the issues I last discussed with him. This allows me to pick up the thread from the previous letter, noting, perhaps, that the student had succeeded in solving one problem I drew his attention to, but not a second one. The strongest essays provoke me to write back to the author about his argument or ideas, whereas the weakest might prompt an explanation about why it is important to write in full sentences.

Because I teach at The Evergreen State College, where grades are not given, I do not need to assign grades to the essays I read. But I always *evaluate* them; I always convey to the student how effective he has been in his writing—how strong or weak a paper he has written. (I think aspiring writers need and want such judgments.)

"Correcting papers" had always been the most onerous teaching task for me. Like most teachers who are saddled with this job, I always dreaded it. Now that I "write letters to students" instead of "correcting their papers," I take some pleasure in the job. It is still time-consuming, and if my students are weak writers, I don't always relish the task. But it is never the ordeal it used to be, now that its spirit has changed.

And the effect of these letters on students is drastically different from that of my old red ink markings. They really do pay attention to what I write now, because I am writing personal letters addressing them as writers; I am not "fixing up" or "defacing" their written products with red ink. The time and thought I put into reading their papers is now apparent to them; before, though I devoted just as much time and thought, it was not. The medium of personal letters makes clear to them that I am taking their writing seriously. This makes a big difference to them. And when a student who turns in a short rush-job discovers that I have written more words in response to his "essay" than the essay itself contains, he usually starts to take his own writing more seriously.

Following are two response letters I have written in recent years. The first is to a student's first essay of the year, on *The Merchant of Venice*.

Dear Mary,

This essay is based on a smart idea and some very good thinking. It is both exciting and frustrating to read—exciting because of the novelty and strength of the ideas, and frustrating because of the incomplete payoff.

I think you are on to something important here and I only wish you would have developed this essay substantially further. Did you really find that two and a half pages were enough to treat it adequately? I can hardly imagine so. You needed twice that much; in five pages, or maybe even four, you could have really made your case much more effectively.

Two things are needed: (1) fuller and clearer explanation of your ideas as you proceed, and (2) more analysis of the play based on your ideas. Most crucially, as you yourself imply, you need a sustained discussion of the climactic (notice the second "c" in that word—"climatic" refers to "climate" not "climax") courtroom scene, one in which you really show how your ideas about the limits of language illuminate the scene.

This is a great start on what could be an excellent essay. Next time, complete the job. I will look forward to reading your next one.

Sincerely,
Don

The second letter responds to a student's second essay of the year, on Plato's *Republic*.

Dear John,

This essay is a substantial improvement over the previous one. It is better written, it is better reasoned, and it is better argued. The distinctive strength of your writing is that you write from conviction and that you write from a somewhat well-established perspective. Both these related factors add energy and interest to your essays. This paper engages the reader, raises many interesting points, and puts your own individual spin on much of the text.

Its central problem is that its argument needs to be extracted and made clearer for the reader. The argument is embedded in the discussions, but it's too much work for the reader to get it out. And you are not really sure, in the end, what you want to argue that Plato is intending. That's part of the problem. You can't really believe he's saying what he's saying, yet you read him saying it over and over.

There is no such word as "its'": there is either "it's" (which only means "it is") and there is "its" (which is the possessive form of "it").

The problem you locate at the end of your paper, and the chief source of your critique, can be resolved by recognizing that Plato proposes two stages of education for his guardians. The first is the nasty one involving all the censorship, and it may be subject to the criticisms you supply; it certainly would be, in Plato's eyes too, if that were all that education consisted of. But the early stages of education described in Books 3–4 are supposed to temper the soul and its parts, especially its appetitive and spirited parts, prior to the appearance of reason. The later education (in Book 7) proceeds through various mathematical sciences and culminates in dialectic—exactly the kind of Socratic inquiry and dialogue that you blame Plato for omitting. Thus, those things that were accepted due to conditioning by the younger child will be subject to rational examination and scrutiny by the mature man or woman—but not until the age of 30! In the earlier parts, Plato is only trying to rein in the appetites before they are susceptible to rational control, so he uses the only thing he thinks he has available: control over the cultural environment that impinges on the child and affects him by example or direct impression (the way music impresses itself on your psyche).

Thus, while not wishing to completely defend the *Republic*'s education plan, I think it is somewhat less unreasonable than you paint it.

Sincerely,
Don

Writing personal letters to students is another way I have discovered to teach with my mouth shut. Though I may write as plainly and bluntly as I wish, I am still writing. My student can read my words in peace and quiet and can decide to do with them what he wishes. He may put them aside or forget them; but because they are down on paper, he may search them out later or stumble upon them by chance. He can show them to his parents or go over them with his friends, and he can write his objections to my comments in the margins of the letter (as it turns out many students do). He can also highlight key sentences, and, if he is really conscientious, he can make an appointment with me, bring the letter with him, and question me about what I wrote. None of these possibilities really exists with criticism delivered aloud.

Converting Lectures into Texts

Lecturing is the quintessential way of teaching through Telling, and as I argued in Chapter 1, most students don't tend to learn much from lectures. But formal talks do have their purposes.

1. They can help students *organize* a great deal of knowledge that they have already learned in a piecemeal fashion.
2. They can generate interest in a new area of study.
3. They can be a way to converse with a colleague in front of students (see Chapter 8).
4. They can allow the teacher to present her own interpretation of course materials to her students.

I would not ban lectures from the classroom; if kept in their place, they can be useful devices.

The word "lecture" originally meant "a reading." In the universities of medieval Europe, before the invention of the printing press, professors would carefully read their lectures verbatim from handwritten manuscripts while students just as carefully copied down their words verbatim. Each student's copy of a course of lectures became his textbook, a valued possession for life. Before the invention of the printing press there was no other efficient way to reproduce written texts for a classroom of students.

In these classes it made sense for students to focus only on careful transcription *during* the lecture; they could read, digest, and think about the content of the lecture later, at their leisure, since they took away from the classroom their own written text of the lecture.

This mode of lecturing, then, is another form of "writing to students." In our electronic age, teachers can eliminate the labor-intensive aspects of the old method of transmission, but retain its spirit and distinctive virtues. There is no need for students to hand copy the words they are listening to. Reproduced copies may be made available to them afterwards.

Construing lectures this way radically shifts the emphasis and purpose of the teacher's efforts. The point now is not to teach through the medium of the spoken word, but to make a written text (which the teacher has composed) available to students for study, and to use the spoken performance merely as a means to interest students in the text. The learning hoped for will take place later, when the student seeks out (or takes out) the written lecture and studies it.

All the virtues of indirect speech listed in the discussion of response letters apply once again in this instance. With a written text of their teacher's words at hand, students can read at their own pace, re-read, stop and take notes, discuss the content with others, and really attend to the *thinking* of their teacher without having to attend to the teacher herself.

Though there are different ways to present such a lecture, formally reading it (rather than engagingly "talking" it) is well-suited to its purpose. A formal reading conveys that the written text is what is important; it helps dispel the illusion that students are actually learning anything by hearing the lecture right there in the room at the moment of its delivery. And it minimizes the misleading effect of the teacher's charisma while maximizing the importance of the teacher's thought expressed in words.

While distributing a copy of the lecture to each student might seem appealing, I prefer to make only a few copies available in the library instead. My hunch is that the sense of security that comes from carrying away the written text is counterproductive. I think the number of students who take the time to read the lecture carefully will be just as great if the lecture is put in the library, and, in the spirit of Plato, I don't wish to foster the illusion that students actually have some knowledge simply because they *possess* a written text. Putting it in the library emphasizes the effort required of students before the written text can become useful to them (and they can make their own personal copies once they get to the library).

Converting lectures into texts will not be an effective way to reach all students, probably not even the majority. But it can be a potent means to reach a few. Its power is maximized by low frequency. Presenting a written text formally should be a special occasion; the less frequently it is done, the more likely students will pay attention to it. And only a well-written text of high quality merits the class time devoted to a formal reading.

This form of lecturing, then, provides another instance of "teaching through writing." The burden of educating, in this instance, is on the teacher's written text, not her spoken delivery. For this reason, it counts as another, though less obvious, form of teaching with your mouth shut.

Writing Essays for Students

The third way to teach through writing is the most straightforward. A teacher may simply write an essay and make it available for students to read. This act is particularly appropriate in an inquiry-centered course (see Chapter 4). Since the teacher is participating along with her students in the inquiry around which the course is organized, it is perfectly appropriate for her to address some aspect of the inquiry by means of an essay. It would be inappropriate to *require* that students read her essays, but it is most reasonable to make them available to those interested.

Writing essays and making them available to students serves three functions: (1) It demonstrates that the teacher is genuinely involved in the inquiry, and that, just as she has asked her students to do, she uses writing as a tool for pursuing the problem at the center of the course. (2) It provides an example of a good essay, one that students might emulate. (3) It *contributes* to the inquiry. It gives the teacher a way of making her own thinking available to the students without forcing it on them. As I have already suggested, a teacher who conveys her ideas to her students by writing to them allows her students to stand on their own two feet in receiving her ideas. In the space opened up between students and teacher, students can carefully read the essay and critically respond to it if they so desire.

Part II: Learning through Writing Together

A Community of Writers

We have seen that students can learn from reading what their teacher has written to them. They can also learn by writing to each other. One of the best ways to make an inquiry-centered course into a genuine *community* of inquiry is to turn it into a "writing community." This organization amplifies all the virtues of pursuing collective inquiry as elaborated in the previous three chapters. Students will talk to each other not only in the classroom but through the exchange of written essays. Their understanding of great books will be advanced by the addition of this "dialogue on paper" about the books. And thus they will be able to push further the inquiry that defines the course.

A writing community will work best in a course if it is buttressed by a classroom context that rests on two assumptions. The first I have already discussed: that the course be conceived as a *locus of intellectual inquiry* (see Chapter 4). The second assumption pertains to writing itself: that the activity of essay writing be understood as a *process of intellectual inquiry*.

These two assumptions taken separately do not quite imply a writing community. One can imagine a course in which students confront problems in an inquiring mode and in which all writing is undertaken as a private transaction between each student and his teacher. Only when a teacher emphasizes the communal side of inquiry and the public character of writing when it serves as a tool of inquiry will she find herself wanting to create a community of writers within a course. Chapter 4 has shown how a course can function as a locus of intellectual inquiry. To see how a writing community can take shape in such a course, we need to examine the second of the two assumptions, that essay writing can be undertaken as a process of intellectual inquiry.

This assumption entails a major shift in the way students think about writing essays. Students have to conceive of writing as "thinking on paper," not just as a means to report the *results* of their thinking, but as a means to extend, develop, refine, and crystallize their thinking. To undertake writing in this spirit, students must begin with a genuine question—one in which they are honestly interested and *to which they do not know the answer when they begin to write their papers*. The teacher must insist on this starting point. Without a genuine question, there is no inquiry to pursue.

Too often students have been taught to begin with a thesis, rather than a question, as if one could have an answer before one had a question. To begin with a thesis means that you have already completed the inquiry before you have started to write. But to begin the writing process with a genuine question is scary; it means starting a paper without knowing whether you will be able to finish it successfully. It takes courage to undertake writing in this spirit, but only by doing so can you use writing to pursue inquiry.

It helps students to distinguish between two stages of writing: discovery and communication. I call them the "path of Discovery" and the "path of Communication" when I discuss this distinction with my students. In pursuing the path of Discovery, you should start with a genuine question, return to the course materials with that question in mind, and write in any format and style that will push your thinking forward. The goal of this work is to *locate your thesis* (i.e., to answer your question).

Once you have found your answer, you have to figure out how to persuade your readers of its soundness. At this point all the rules of essay writing come into play, rules that require logical argument, effective organization, and clear writing. But it makes no sense to work on effective communication if you haven't made any discoveries worth communicating.

For most students, pursuing their essay writing in the spirit of inquiry requires a major shift of gears. The change doesn't come automatically, but if their teacher relentlessly persists in demanding that they start with a genuine question, they eventually get the idea. And once they start writing in this spirit, they find essay writing to be integral to their studies—not just to yield final products of learning but as an indispensable tool in getting to those final products.

Several years ago, I taught a course called *"Polis" and Psyche,* an inquiry-based course described briefly at the end of Chapter 4. I advertised the course as a community of writers. Structuring the course so that students felt themselves to be members of a writing community rather than disconnected students writing for a single teacher entailed making two fundamental changes in their approach to writing.

First, I had to get the students to undertake writing as a process of inquiry in the manner just described. Second, I had to get them to undertake writing as a process of *public* and *collective* inquiry. That meant getting the students to write *for each other* rather than just for me; it meant getting the students to use their essays as a vehicle for sharing with each other the results of their inquiries into the books they were reading.

In practice, this shift necessitated two specific changes in student behavior: (1) the students had to read each other's essays; and (2) they had to provide written responses to those essays. This second activity gave them the opportunity to *receive* written responses from their peers, as well. The sum of these changes was to create an ongoing dialogue on paper about the course materials to complement the spoken dialogue that took place in the continual class discussions.

The logistics for bringing about these changes were as follows:

1. Students wrote essays every other week, due at the end of the week.

2. These essays were officially handed in, not to the teacher, but to a Class Notebook, which the teacher brought to class every other Friday, but which was normally kept on the Open Reserve shelf in the college library.

3. A *copy* of the essay was given to the teacher to read and evaluate.

4. During the alternate weeks when no essays were due, each student was required to read through the Class Notebook, select two "interesting" essays, and, for each, write a letter to its author responding critically to the essay. My specific instructions were:

   These should be letters responding to the thinking in the papers, not an English teacher's picky responses to the technicalities of writing. However, form and content are ultimately inseparable in writing, and it is appropriate and helpful to comment on aspects of the writing that interfere with (or enhance) your understanding of the paper's substance.

5. These letters were produced in triplicate. One copy went directly to the essay's author, a second went into the Class Notebook following the essay it addressed, and a third was submitted to me. I read these letters, verifying that they were written, but did not evaluate or return them.

6. Students were free to choose whichever essays and whichever authors they wished to respond to. I imposed no restrictions to equalize the number of authors addressed. That meant that some students received many more letters than others did. The students thus faced an ongoing reality-test with regard to their writing; each essay received a tangible measure of how interesting it was: the number of letters received in response. On the other hand, students did base their selection on grounds other than pure "interest." In general, they spread their responses around, not so much to be fair, but because they were genuinely interested in what most of their classmates thought about the material. (This structure was particularly effective in giving students access to the thinking of the "quieter students," peers whose views they would otherwise have no clue about.)

7. Finally, I evaluated each student's essay by means of a personal letter of the type discussed in Part I of this chapter. These letters were often quite lengthy, and were written with energy and feeling. In form and detail these letters did not, as one might have expected, serve as a model for the letters that students wrote. But the dedication and hard work that so clearly lay behind them did serve an exemplary purpose. While certainly every student did not follow my example, nevertheless my letters affected in a salutary way the whole spirit in which response letter writing was undertaken. Nothing could have better conveyed to the students the seriousness with which I took their writing than my letters in response to them, and even though these were private and did not appear in the Notebook, their effect on the public spirit of writing in the course was far from negligible.

Writing for a Genuine Audience

These changes really do alter the intellectual environment of the classroom. All their lives students have written for teachers, and teachers only. Suddenly they are writing for a wider audience, a genuine audience—their friends and fellow students. Because these are the people participating with them in a common inquiry, they are the audience it makes sense to write to. These are their colleagues. Their concern for their teacher's approval of their writing does not, of course, disappear; but it is now coupled with, and in some cases overshadowed by, their equally serious concern with their essays' reception by their peers. These colleagues are engaged in studying the same materials and thinking about the same problems; their judgments matter.

One student, when asked about the impact of writing to her classmates, remarked, "Writing for the teacher, you can slack off a little, but writing for everyone, you can't." She went on to mention a surprising effect of the writing community arrangement: "There's not one person you're trying to please, so you end up doing it for yourself."

Knowing that their essays are going to be read by their classmates, students discover a reality-base for their writing that is absent in most school writing. When a student writes an essay that will be read by *only one person,* and when that one person is his *teacher,* and when the teacher's main reason for reading the paper is to *judge* the quality of the writing, the student is engaging in a triply unnatural act. We write to communicate our ideas, as well as to give them shape. When we write formally, we typically address an audience of more than a single reader. And we write to affect our readers' views, to shape their thinking—not to receive a grade from them.

Creating a community of writers in a course does not eliminate the unnaturalness of writing to a teacher who will judge your work, but it balances this aspect of the experience by creating a broader purpose for the writing, one that restores the intrinsic aim of writing. The judging teacher becomes just one reader in a larger audience; her reaction still counts, but it is no longer the only one that counts.

Making students write to each other also provides a strong way to help students pursue inquiry within a course. Their essays become both means and ends: *means* for pushing their thinking, testing their ideas, reaching conclusions, and *ends* as published accounts of their conclusions, which can be read by their classmates. Once read by the class, the essays turn back into means again, because now they function as provocations to the thinking of others.

An additional benefit of this set-up is that by writing response letters to each other, students get to produce public writing that is *not* formally evaluated; they get to write informally and spontaneously about academic issues without having to worry about form and "correctness." The repeated activity of this kind of writing helps them get used to "thinking on paper" and often provides fertile ground for engendering ideas that can later be used in their formal essays.

To give the flavor of student response letters, I include here some letters and excerpts written by students from *In Search of Socrates,* another course organized as a writing community. The following letter is shorter than the average response letter—and also somewhat more lively.

Dear Peter,

Let me just say now that I have enjoyed all of your papers, even though I have waited till now to respond to you. You're a great writer. And I especially liked this one.

Right here baby: "It wasn't that Socrates failed to love. His love failed. Perhaps any love would have failed." I just love that. How the hell can anybody save mankind from greed, pride, and false knowledge? Anyone who has had this mission in life has been a complete failure. But, of course, I chose to interpret Socrates as not even really trying; I like to see him mainly concerned with saving himself.

I also really like your explanation of Socrates' "versatility of voice." The dialogues are really dramas. They are not straight, dry philosophical discussions, but stories with friendships and tensions and emotions. When Socrates speaks, it is somehow clear that he is trying to convey something more than just what his words say; he is a human being relating to other human beings on many different levels. It is obvious that he is up to something when he talks. He lies, or exaggerates, regularly, and we never really know when he is telling the truth. So it's almost impossible to tell what this "something" that he is up to is. Anyway, I liked all the adjectives you wrote that could be used to describe him.

Lastly, the unfinished painting metaphor was wonderful. It is always open to a few drastic changes, and you are always in it. Socrates will change you. I like a paper that ends in flux. Change, you're beautiful. (You know how people say, "Don't change, you're beautiful"?)

Sincerely,
Eliot

Here are the opening paragraphs of three more student response letters from this course.

My dear David,

Well, I must say, after our many mirrored strides in the philosophical inquiry together, it is really refreshing to disagree with you. Well, at least I thought that at first (if you recall the stance I took in my paper), but now I am wondering what your paper is really saying about your understanding of that mythological Socrates.

Rebecca,

I had fun reading your work. You painted an interesting portrait of Socrates and gave me a new sense of his mission. But your essay left me with a lot of questions. You seem to make Socrates into someone hell-bent on an agenda and opportunistic enough to use any means available for furthering his plan.

Dear Fred,

Your opening paragraph left me gaping. I found myself staring, eyes wide, thinking, "Oh my, really?" At this point I found it impossible to put your paper down.

The response letters also become a vehicle of expression (as do the formal essays) for students who are not comfortable speaking in class. With a class organized as a community of writers, the "quiet" students are no longer relegated to the "second-class citizen" status that discussion-based courses inevitably confer upon them. They have an outlet for their own ideas about the material and an avenue for expressing their reactions to others' ideas. They become respected members of the class. Here is a letter written by a quiet student (*to* a quiet student).

Dear Martha,

You've given me a lot to think about.

I liked your conclusion that Socrates was asserting individuality over plurality. It makes sense to me, but now I'm going to have to rethink my interpretations of all of the dialogues. It would certainly clear up a lot of the seminar discussions dealing with whether Socrates was pro aristocracy or pro democracy.

Your paper also gave me an idea—which may be reading between the lines on my part—because you don't come out and state it. The idea is that politics may not be a separate art or field of study, but something inherent in human nature. Politics is an extrapolation of our day-to-day relationships. This means we are all experts, if we inquire into our own actions. I don't know—I see holes all through that argument.

I refused to write on Nietzsche or Stone because I disagreed with their views. Now I'm not so sure. Great paper!

Sincerely,
Scott

Finally, here is what one student wrote to me in a faculty evaluation about his experience as a member of a writing community.

But the true and simple stroke of genius . . . was your requirement (not invitation, but requirement) that we read each other's essays and respond to our classmates in writing through that archaic and underestimated tool known as the letter. Don, this humble idea . . . was one of the most powerful choices I've ever seen a teacher make. This decentralized the whole writing event: my audience was real, immediate, and critical; I was a writer in a community of writers; my writing had an impact on other people's inquiry and on the seminar as a whole; I was not alone writing at a college that doesn't give grades—I was working cooperatively with my colleagues around a shared question. The exchange of letters was central to the cultivation of a pro-intellectual climate; I've never felt so generous towards others in an academic setting and I've never felt other people work so hard for me. The feedback I received from classmates _____ and _____, among others, was very insightful and had a real impact on my writing process and on the final product that fell out of that process. I met people through the exchange of letters who I just wouldn't have talked to in another environment (sad to say, but that's the truth). . . . I leave this class with a reverence for something that today's world tells us is obsolete and I now hold as essential: the exchange of letters.

Speaking with Your Mouth Shut

By organizing her class as a community of writers, a teacher provides another way for students to learn from each other. They learn from each other by writing together: by writing essays to each other, reading each other's essays, thinking critically about the essays they have read, and then by writing letters back to the essays' authors. All this activity happens while the teacher is keeping her own mouth shut.

If, at the same time, the teacher puts her own pen into motion, joining the community of writers by becoming a writer herself (in one of the ways mentioned in Part I of this chapter), then her teaching becomes doubly powerful. In the first place, she has the opportunity to influence her students' thinking through the indirect art of writing. In the second place, she legitimizes, grounds, and enriches the writing community itself by becoming an active member of it. Her participation will lead the students to take it all the more seriously.

In this way, the activities described separately in the two parts of this chapter fall naturally together into one whole. A community of inquiry in which writing is taken to be just as inevitable and important as reading and discussing becomes a powerful place of learning. It is a place where a teacher can do much to assist her students, even though she refrains from telling them what they should know. By keeping her mouth shut, she makes room for two more teaching activities that will help her students learn: She can arrange for them to write to each other, and she can write to them herself. By doing the former, she invites *them* to speak with their mouths shut. By doing the latter, she shows them how to do it.

6

Experiences That Teach
Creating Blueprints for Learning

Putting the Teacher's Thinking at the Students' Disposal

In Chapter 4, I said that one of my five jobs as the teacher of an inquiry-centered course was putting my own thinking at the students' disposal. I do this job primarily through classroom exercises called "conceptual workshops." I alluded to these exercises in Chapter 3 when referring to "in-class study groups," student groups that form for one class period to work on written problems given them by the teacher.

Writing focused, directed problems and getting students to work on them in small groups is another way to teach with your mouth shut. Yet it is a kind of teaching that differs distinctly from any we have examined so far. The teacher aims to make her students learn by designing an experience that will teach them. To understand how she can do this, we must return to the "perplexing problem" or "puzzle," a learning scenario we passed over quickly in Chapter 2.

What Happens When the Canary Takes Off?

A canary is standing on the bottom of a very large sealed bottle that is placed on a scale. The bird takes off and flies around the inside of the bottle. What happens to the reading of the scale? Explain.

I presented this question as an example of a puzzle or perplexing problem after the discussion of parables in Chapter 2. At that time, I suggested that you take a moment to think about it. If you did not do so then, please stop reading now and think about how you would answer the question. What do you think will happen to the reading of the scale when the canary takes flight inside the bottle? Will it drop? Will it stay the same? Will it shift more than once? What will happen?

Designing an Experience that Teaches

Most people find this a challenging problem. They find that it engages their intuitions about weight, gravity, and other physical forces. At the same time, it destabilizes their thinking about these ideas, upsetting their mental balance. However they wish to answer the question initially, they are forced to question their own answer and think further. Precisely for these reasons, the puzzle stimulates their curiosity and energizes their thinking. In the language of Chapter 4, it creates a "present interest," a need to know which originates in our automatic tendency to restore a disturbed equilibrium.

The canary problem can be a useful teaching device, a text that provokes curiosity in students and puts their minds in motion. But the canary problem, all by itself, is not likely to sustain inquiry for long. If a student becomes stumped, there is nothing in the problem to get him over his obstacle. And if he does not find the problem all that interesting, there is nothing in it to get him interested.

Let us therefore try to add some features to the canary problem, and by this means build up an organized set of activities around it to remedy these deficiencies. Starting with this puzzling problem, we will add one factor after another, and in this way gradually turn it into a sustained learning activity. Thus, instead of just *hoping* that students have the kind of instructive experience encountering the problem that we envisage, we will *design an environment*—with the puzzle at its center—that makes that experience much more likely. We can't force the experience to come about, but we can increase its probability dramatically.

Other People to Talk To

The first thing someone puzzling about the canary needs is other people to talk to. So we will give him three companions and pose the canary problem to the group of four, asking them to agree on an answer. Making the problem a group problem has four important consequences.

1. Working with others requires each student to voice his own ideas aloud. This process of articulation does more than just translate what is inside his head to the outside world. It forces him to *improve* the

quality of what is inside his head: In giving words to his ideas, he must clarify them, distinguish them, give them shape. In addition, giving voice to his ideas allows him to know what he thinks. This may sound strange, but we often do not know what we think until we hear what we say. We are too close to the thoughts inside our own head to get any distance, and our unvoiced ideas are often too fuzzy and indistinct to be readily grasped. Putting our thoughts into words both forces them to take on a more distinct shape *and* allows us to become acquainted with them. So, even if his three companions never say a word, they help the student considerably by becoming an audience to his thinking.

2. But, of course, they will say something. And so their second contribution is the obvious one of presenting new ideas and perspectives on the problem. Two heads are better than one, and four are usually better than two.

3. But even if their ideas are no better than his own, hearing them is likely to provoke new ideas in our original student. Ideas are not static entities that collect in a room; they have a dynamic effect upon one another. They interact not like marbles, but like chemicals; their interaction can bring about the creation of something new. And that is the third contribution of making the problem a group one. Together, the group can develop new ideas that no single group member could have devised on his own.

4. Finally, the presence of the group creates motivation. Encountering the problem alone, unless constrained by external rewards or punishments, a student will be moved to think about it to the extent that he finds his curiosity stimulated. But the minute he is part of a group that has been handed the task of solving the problem, he finds other people depending on his assistance. Most people respond to the unspoken pull of group norms. Thus, he is more likely to make a genuine effort to solve the problem as a group member than as a solitary individual.

A Sequence of Questions That Build

The next thing needed is a sequence of questions to follow up on the canary problem. The group working on the problem needs someplace to go. If they cannot solve the problem correctly, they need further activities to help them reorganize their thinking. And even if they do solve it correctly, they are not likely to be certain of their solution. They need a way to test their thinking and to stabilize the ideas that led to the correct solution.

Moreover, we have no guarantee that the group will genuinely come to agree about the effect on the scale of the canary's flight. We have asked them to agree, but they may not be able to. And even if a nominal agreement is reached, shyer or more polite participants may have suppressed their own convictions in the interest of group harmony. The group needs to work further in order to attain genuine understanding.

So we, who know the correct answer and understand the reasons behind it, must design a series of questions to follow up on the initial problem. These questions will provide guidance in solving the problem without providing an answer. They will give the students direction without taking over the job of thinking for them.

The following question makes a good follow-up to the canary problem:

> A goldfish is lying on the bottom of a large goldfish bowl filled with water that is placed on a scale. The fish takes off and swims around the inside of the bowl. What happens to the reading of the scale? Explain.

This problem is clearly related to the first one. It is similar in structure, yet different in some crucial details. We have swimming instead of flying, we have water instead of air, and we have a bowl open at the top to the surrounding environment. Do any of these changes affect the answer to the question? What is the effect of all of them in combination? That is what the group members will debate with each other.

This second question is helpful because it asks the same question about a situation that is similar to the first one yet transformed in certain crucial ways. Sustaining a train of thought across a transformation is the most useful way to test it, to sharpen it, and to stabilize it. That is why this question is useful regardless of whether the group answered the first question correctly or not.

The goldfish problem not only poses a second question, but inevitably provokes a reconsideration of the first question. That is its first virtue. That is why we say it "follows up on" or "builds upon" the first question. We are not really asking a sequence of isolated questions; we are using a sequence of questions to stimulate a single process of inquiry into a dynamic situation involving a number of physical concepts (mass, the force of gravity, air pressure).

The second virtue of the goldfish problem is that it engages a second set of intuitions about the interaction of weight, force, and motion in a physical medium. These intuitions are likely to lead many people to a different hunch about the answer than they had in response to the canary problem. This outcome indicates that their intuitions about the two different situations were not in contact with each other. By posing *this* particular question about a goldfish directly after *that* particular question about a canary, we forcibly bring the two sets of intuitions into proximity. For many, this new contact will create a sense of self-contradiction. Both intuitions seem right in isolation, but taking them together leads to a third intuition: They both can't be right. Or can they? The sense of a contradiction could be unfounded, but even if it is, it demands an explanation. Thus, the group may find itself discussing why the two situations, which seem similar, really are different. And so different answers may be justified. This is just the kind of discussion we want.

Thinking out loud together in this manner, the group is likely to progress. Even if they move away from a correct answer to the canary problem toward an incorrect one, they are making progress because they are *thinking*. They have located concepts in their minds, oiled them up, and gotten them moving by applying them to a particular concrete problem. They may be making new distinctions, new connections, or both. If their motion is in the right direction, we want them to move further in that direction. If their motion is in an incorrect direction, we want them to run up against further problems so that—through their own thinking—they will discover their mistake and change directions. In either case, their minds must become active. But also, in either case, more questions that continue building on the first two will be needed to advance the process we have begun with the canary and the goldfish.

By transforming the air in the canary's bottle to the water in the goldfish's bowl, we have forced attention on the medium in which each creature moves, and the mechanisms by which each counteracts the force of gravity when it leaves the floor of its container. Can we go further in this same direction by making these same aspects of the problem even more obvious? We can. We can do so with the following two questions (now numbered to make explicit their place in the sequence).

3. A man is standing on a scale. He then gets off the scale, places a large metal spiral spring (as large as he is) on the scale, and stands on top of the spring. What happens to the reading of the scale? Explain. (For simplicity's sake, ignore the weight of the spring itself in answering this question.)

4. Suppose the man above replaces the spring on the scale by an "air spring." This is a cylinder (as large as the man) with a piston that slides down into it. There is a column of air trapped in the cylinder, and the man stands on a platform mounted atop the piston. The cylinder is open at the bottom, but is connected to the scale by an air-tight seal. Compare the scale readings when the man is on the air-spring as opposed to when he is directly on the scale. Explain. (Once again, ignore the weight of the air-spring itself.)

With the addition of these questions we now have a somewhat complete and satisfying sequence of four questions that build upon each other in a consistent way. Notice, however, that they do not build in the manner of a mathematical proof or a logical argument. They build in a completely different manner. They build by carefully drawing together experiences familiar to the participants and ideas they already have for explaining those experiences. None of these ideas, taken individually, is new. What is new here is that they have never been brought together and never been made to reconcile with each other.

We all have unexamined "theories" about what makes scales register, what makes fish swim, how birds fly, and how pistons push. These "theories" range from vague intuitions to clear and well-articulated concepts—most tending to the former. Rarely in everyday life are they put to the test. Our sequence of questions not only puts them to the test one at a time, but, because it *is* a sequence, asks the students to come up with one consistent theory to explain all four situations. To succeed at this task, they have to re-construct their thinking—take their ideas apart and put them back together again differently. This is precisely the process that leads to understanding, and hence to knowledge.

Our sequence of questions also works by focusing attention on *specific aspects* of the problem. The original canary problem presents a perplexing question and leaves you alone to grapple with it as you will. But the minute we add the goldfish problem to it, we have asked you to focus on certain dimensions of the problem (those that the two problems have in common or those on which the two problems differ strikingly) and to ignore other aspects (those that fall into neither of these two categories). Thus, you are virtually forced to focus on the physical medium (air or water) and on the forces by means of which the two creatures propel themselves upward in their respective media. On the other hand, you are not likely to worry about the different shapes of the two animals, or their different colors, or the fact that one survives in air and the other dies in air.

Our sequence of questions, though coherent and satisfying, is not yet complete. The third and fourth questions construct increasingly artificial situations in order to focus and direct the thinking of the group. But by the time we get to the stationary man standing on the air-spring, we have traveled quite a distance from the spontaneous canary in flight. Another question, or sub-sequence of questions, is needed both to make sure that the man and the canary remain connected and to deal with the problems created by the artificiality of the man on the air-spring and the counter-intuitive nature of the correct answer to the original canary problem (see below). Here is a sub-sequence that will help.

5. (a) In the canary problem in 1, suppose the bottle is replaced by a cage that is mostly glass, but with very thin spaces between the glass bars. What happens?

   (b) Suppose it is replaced by an ordinary wire cage?

   (c) Suppose the bird is hovering over the scale and is not enclosed at all?

   (d) What if the bird simply flies over the scale? Discuss.

We have assumed all along that our sequence of questions leads the students to think about the separate problems together. Question 5(a) makes sure they do. By returning to the caged canary, it gets the students to apply their current thinking about the man on the air-spring back to the original canary problem. In order to secure this connection, they will inevitably work their way backwards and forwards through the sequence: man-on-air-spring, man-on-metal-spring, goldfish-in-water, and canary-in-air. Question 5(a) thus deals with the problem of the distance traversed going from the canary to the air-spring and pushes the students to come up with one unified "theory" to account for all four cases.

If they succeed, they will have discovered that the scale reading in the sealed bottle with the bird flying around inside it reads just the same as it does with the bird standing on the floor of the bottle. For the bird to stay aloft, the moving molecules of air that hold it up must push down on the scale with just the same force as the bird originally did (the force caused by the pull of gravity on the bird's mass). This explanation works well to explain and harmonize the four cases (and is correct), but there may still be a nagging problem. The correct answer seems to suggest that if a bird in free flight flew over a bathroom scale, the reading on the scale would shoot up for a second (as the bird flew directly over the scale) and then drop back to zero—and we *know* that wouldn't happen (Don't we?)

So a secondary problem is created: How do we reconcile one "correct" answer we have figured out from a series of artificially constructed problems with a contradictory "correct" answer that we know from our everyday experience? The final sub-sequence is designed to stimulate a small process of thinking to reconcile the two "correct" answers. It turns out that the difference made by the *sealed* bottle in the original problem is crucial, and it is not hard to see why. The sub-sequence, in perhaps more detail than is necessary, will help almost anyone see why—and thus provides a satisfactory conclusion to the main sequence. Now our explanation of the canary problem fits not only with the other scenarios but also with common sense and everyday experience. We are ready to take a well-deserved break.

(For the reader's convenience, I have assembled the five questions, which I will henceforth call "the Canary Problem," in an Appendix to this chapter.)

A Teacher to Call On

The problems described in this chapter teach by their very structure. They don't Tell directly. Rather they encourage the making of discoveries. They create an intellectual environment with a shape—an environment with constraints, demands, orientations, limits, opportunities, and invitations (see Chapter 7)—and they set the students free in it. They don't do the necessary thinking for the students and announce the results. They require the students to think for themselves, to find their own results, and then to test them in new circumstances. In this way, they lead to learning that lasts.

By designing these questions and setting them before a group of students, we have served as their teacher. We have taught them something significant about matter and motion in a physical medium. A teacher who teaches by designing such questions is teaching with her mouth shut. Instead of telling her students what she wants them to know, she designs an *experience* for them—one that will engender, she hopes, the understanding she wishes her students to achieve.

A teacher cannot actually engineer an experience, however. The best she can do is to shape an environment for students so that, once students are set free in it, the experience she hopes for is likely to result.

The most crucial aspect of this environment is the sequence of the questions themselves. (I take for granted more obvious though necessary features of the environment: a well-lit, heated, quiet physical space conducive to intellectual work, chairs that can be arranged in small circles, enough space so the students can talk without being distracted by neighboring groups, and so forth.) We have already discussed a second feature of the intellectual environment—the presence of other students. By supplying the written questions and the other students, the teacher has done the lion's share of her teaching. But her work is not over. We are ready to add a third feature to our original scenario (the solitary canary problem): a teacher to call on.

The sequence of problems and the accompanying instructions must be *written out and distributed to every student* (for reasons we shall examine later). While *necessary*, this condition is not *sufficient* for generating the kind of experience we are after. Like the best-laid plans of mice, a teacher's instructions do not always achieve their desired results, be they ever so clearly written out. So the teacher herself must be available in the room when the students are working.

Inevitably, questions will be misunderstood, instructions will be ignored or misconstrued, digressions will materialize. Beyond these obvious obstacles to learning lies a second set. All student groups will not run smoothly. Some will be dominated by one or two strong members. Some will suffer from an absence of any assertive members. Some will be led astray by misguided "authorities." And beyond this set of problems lies a third: the intellectual work itself may lead to tangles or dead ends. The questions are designed to point in a specific direction, but they cannot guarantee what direction any particular group will take. Like a computer program still in need of debugging, a group can land itself in a closed loop, energetically and endlessly discussing something that leads nowhere.

In all these cases and more, the presence of a roving teacher, quietly monitoring the discussion groups, can make the crucial difference. The teacher will tell the groups at the start to feel free to call her over if they get stuck or need help. In addition, she will wander around, sitting in (not hovering over) one group at a time, listening to their discussion, intervening only if she thinks help is needed (and then briefly), and then departing to visit another group.

There is no recipe for the teacher to follow, but in most cases what is called for will be obvious. And in some cases, simple Telling may be what is called for. "The air serves the same purpose for the bird as the water does for the fish." "The air in the air-spring won't hold the man up unless it is pushing down on something." But even in these cases, the Telling is brief, it occasions further inquiry, and it is tailored to the specific obstacles blocking four people discussing the problem. It doesn't turn their minds off and transform them into passive listeners to a lecture. It removes a glitch that has blocked the forward motion of their minds and gets them moving again.

The teacher's discreet but active physical presence in the environment is a crucial addition to our original scenario. She will find scores of different functions to perform, and each will be honed to the specific problem that has cropped up for four specific people. She is an important part of the environment she has created for her students but also a small part. She is more like a roving auto mechanic than an actor. Or, to stick with the theater, we may consider her a stage manager. She sets the stage and removes obstructions so that the play can proceed. (She is a stage manager *during* the play, but she has also written the script. She accomplished that work before she ever came to class—and in striking contrast to a lecturer, *she* is not the one who has to perform the script.)

An Ending to the Experience

In his definition of tragedy in the *Poetics,* Aristotle requires of that theatrical experience that it be (among other things) "whole." "A whole," says Aristotle, "is that which has a beginning, a middle, and an end." An intellectual experience ought to be whole, too. If we aim to *design* a sustained learning experience for students, we will do well to give that experience some organic shape through time: We need to provide a beginning, a middle, and an end.

In the experience we have been designing, the original canary problem constitutes the beginning. It presents a concrete, easily understood set of circumstances and poses a perplexing question about it. The initial question engages the student, creating "present interest" and a motivation to proceed further. When we get to the goldfish, we have entered the middle phase, and we stay in this phase through our encounter with the man on the air-spring. Question 5, with its sub-sequence of questions, provides an ending. The sub-sequence is designed to satisfy any lingering doubts, to integrate the conclusions produced from all preceding questions, and to provide a sense of intellectual closure.

Question 5 provides an ending to the *intellectual* side of the experience, but there is a *social* side to the experience as well, and a teacher neglects it at her peril. If you have been one of four students working on problems your teacher has prescribed to you in a room filled with many other groups of students working on the same problems, you are aware of yourself as part of a complex social arrangement. Before you are done, you would like to know what conclusions the other groups came to, how these compared with your group's, what your teacher thinks of all these conclusions—and what, after all, are the right answers anyway.

To make the experience whole, we need to give it a more comprehensive and satisfying ending. That is the fourth and final feature we need to transform our original perplexing problem into a sustained learning experience.

There are many ways to create an ending, just as there are many ways to shape intellectual experiences as a whole. The simplest and most straightforward is to allow some time at the end when each group can report the results of its investigations, these results can be compared, discussion can take place stimulated by divergent results, and the teacher can comment on what she has seen happening, as briefly or as fully, as directly or as indirectly, as she deems wise.

Providing an ending to the *immediate* experience that day in class, however, in no way implies shutting off further exploration of the problem or the issues underlying it. If the Canary Problem were included in an inquiry-centered course (see Chapter 4), its teacher would certainly be committed to *continuing* the inquiry beyond the boundaries of one class day. The last thing she would desire would be to end it. But a commitment to ongoing inquiry does not do away with the need to provide emotional closure and a sense of an ending to the immediate experience. If you put students to work on a challenging problem for a sustained period of time, if you force them to struggle and sweat, then you owe it to them to create an ending. An ending will not only give them a sense of intrinsic satisfaction (because the experience will feel, to some degree, completed), but it will give them a chance to get some distance on their work, to reflect on it, and thus to take more away from it.

Conceptual Workshops

We started with an engaging puzzle, the canary problem, and in four steps we converted it into a sustained learning experience for students. We added (a) other people to talk to, (b) a sequence of questions that built on the original question, (c) a teacher to call on, and (d) an ending to the experience. By developing the canary problem in this way, we have provided ourselves with one image of an "experience that teaches." At the same time, we have gotten a sense of what might be involved in a teacher's designing such an experience. But a single example is always misleading. It will be helpful to look at another.

Before doing so, let us establish some terminology and examine the classroom context for these learning activities. The teaching approach exemplified by the Canary Problem was developed by a former colleague (Stephen Monk) and me in the early '70s. It started as an attempt to promote more active learning for students in the large lecture courses we both taught at that time. We designated the approach as "the design of intellectual experience" and we characterized the teachers' challenge as "turning the products of their academic disciplines back into the processes that led to them." This language seems just as appropriate today as it did twenty-five years ago.

But we never came up with a suitable short name for the kinds of classes we were designing nor for the materials necessary to run them. We ended up relying on the vague but convenient terms *workshops* and *worksheets.* The latter were the written handouts containing the questions and instructions, and the former were the classes themselves: A workshop was a class in which a teacher distributed a worksheet and her students followed the instructions on it.

The problem is that for more than twenty-five years, and ever more increasingly, the term *workshop* has been used to designate every kind of activity imaginable—including sessions where experts are brought in to do nothing more than lecture to professionals on some special topic. The word has become virtually meaningless. Yet it is hard to give up: It retains its appeal through its connotations of active learning and its echoes of "the lab" and of John Dewey's "lab schools." But the term will not suffice without further specification.

Of late, I have come to call these classes "conceptual workshops." This phrase emphasizes the conceptual nature of both the learning aimed for and the work required of the workshop's designer. I shall continue using the term *worksheets,* hoping that my context indicates that these are the materials necessary to run "conceptual workshops."

The Classroom Context

A conceptual workshop typically runs for two to three hours (with breaks), but may range from fifty minutes to four hours. (Long ones may be broken up into segments and conducted on successive days, if necessary.) Students do most of the work in small groups, but some of the tasks may be undertaken individually and some by the class as a whole.

The size of the small group will depend on the teacher's judgment of the optimal size for pursuing the work demanded by her worksheet. In the course of one conceptual workshop, students may participate in several different groups, small groups may join together to form larger groups, large groups may split up into smaller ones, or phases of individual and group work may follow each other repeatedly. However, the typical format is the simple one in which students divide into groups of about four, work for a fairly long time on a sequence of questions, and then discuss the results of their work with the rest of the students in the class.

The teacher conducts the workshop simply by handing out a copy of the worksheet to every student and telling them to get started. She then roams from group to group, listening to the discussions, and intervening when her words will advance (and not obstruct!) the activities the worksheet was written to promote. If there is a final discussion, she will conduct it, participating in it as she sees fit.

Teachers who intend to use conceptual workshops do well to use them regularly. As a one-time activity in a course where different styles of teaching and learning are the norm, a conceptual workshop is not apt to succeed. Students need to become accustomed to the different kinds of demands these classes make on them, to the different rhythm of work, and the different classroom atmosphere. They also need to get a taste of their distinct intellectual rewards. It does not take long for all these things to happen, but it does take *some* time. I typically employ conceptual workshops once a week; others might opt for using them every second or third week (they take quite some time to prepare). But even if they occur as seldom as once every three weeks, students—adaptive creatures that they are—will have no trouble shifting gears appropriately on "workshop days," once they have gotten some experience with them (*and* if they are convinced that the hard work demanded of them will pay off both in their learning and in their grades).

I never grade or evaluate the work students produce in the workshops themselves. I believe that students must be free to make mistakes without consequences while they are learning, and thus I hold off on evaluation until the end of a learning sequence. I also never ask students to submit what they write during conceptual workshops, though some teachers might wish to. I always feel that I have learned more than enough about their thinking (*and* about what needs revising in my worksheet) by listening in on the group discussions during the workshop itself.

"Aporia"

In Search of Socrates, the inquiry-centered course described in Chapter 4, relies heavily on conceptual workshops. On a typical week, I conduct two of them, a long workshop on Monday and a shorter one on Friday. The following worksheet is from one of the Friday workshops. I designed it to illustrate one concept central to the understanding of Socrates' manner of pursuing philosophy. By the time they get to this workshop, the students have already read and discussed the dialogues referred to in the first question, as well as Aristophanes' satire of Socrates, the *Clouds.* As you read through the worksheet, envision yourself as one of six students in a discussion group. Try to imagine the kind of experience you would be likely to have with five classmates—all of you interested in Socrates—as you spend ninety minutes attempting to answer the questions.

IN SEARCH OF SOCRATES
Spring 1995
FRIDAY WORKSHOP: *"Aporia"*

Part I (70 minutes): Divide into groups of six. Limit discussion of each question to about ten minutes.

Each group should try to agree on an answer to each question. Select one person ahead of time to write down the agreed-upon answer. If agreement cannot be reached in the allotted time, then the scribe should record the dissenting views as well. Select a second person at the start to keep an eye on the time and to make sure the group proceeds through the worksheet in a timely manner.

1. Consider six "moments" in a dialogue with Socrates, each drawn from a different dialogue:
   a. From *Laches* (194a–b), Laches says, "I am ready to go on, Socrates, and yet I am unused to investigations of this sort. But the spirit of controversy has been aroused in me by what has been said, and I am really grieved at being thus unable to express my meaning. For I fancy that I do know the nature of courage, but, somehow or other, she has slipped away from me, and I cannot get hold of her and tell her nature."
   b. From *Euthyphro,* (11b), Euthyphro says, "Now, Socrates, I simply don't know how to tell you what I think. Somehow everything that we put forward keeps moving about us in a

circle, and nothing will stay where we put it."

c. From *Republic* I (334c), Polemarchus says, "No, by Zeus, I no longer know what I did mean. Yet this I still believe, that justice benefits the friends and harms the enemies."

d. From *Crito* (50a), Crito says, "I can't answer your question, Socrates. I am not clear in my mind."

e. From Xenophon, *Recollections* (IV.2.19), p. 111, Euthydemus says, "Socrates, I really don't trust my own answers any longer. Everything that I said before now seems to be different from what I once thought."

f. From *Meno* (80a–b), Meno says to Socrates, "At this moment I feel you are exercising magic and witchcraft upon me and positively laying me under your spell until I am just a mass of helplessness. If I may be flippant, I think that not only in outward appearance but in other respects as well you are exactly like the flat sting ray that one meets in the sea. Whenever anyone comes into contact with it, it numbs him, and that is the sort of thing that you seem to be doing to me now. My mind and my lips are literally numb, and I have nothing to reply to you."

What is similar about these six moments? Formulate a paragraph describing what has happened at this point in the dialogue to the person conversing with Socrates.

2. There is a Greek word to describe this state. The word is *aporia*. Scholars of Plato use this word to describe moments such as these. Rather than defining it formally, it is best to define it inductively as you have just done, looking at the moments of *aporia* and trying to capture what they share in common.

In an article entitled, "Aristophanes and Socrates on learning practical wisdom" (*Yale Classical Studies,* Vol. XXVI, 1980, p. 75), Martha Nussbaum writes, "The paralyzing effect of the *elenchos* [refutation] . . . finds its comic expression in the *Clouds* in the scene in which Strepsiades, enjoined to look into himself and find a solution to his *aporia,* feels himself being bitten by bedbugs that drink his life's blood and torture his genitals." Taking into account Aristophanes' penchant for extreme exaggeration and coarse caricature, do you think the scene where Strepsiades is tortured by bedbugs in his mattress reflects the state of *aporia* as you have conceived it above?

3. Go back to the texts and locate each of the six moments of *aporia*. For each one locate and describe *what Socrates does* in response

to each of these six moments. Just find out literally what happens next in the dialogue and describe it. (In two of the six cases, the answer will be: Socrates just goes on with the argument; the other four cases are more interesting.)

4. In each of the four "interesting" cases, Socrates does something different, but is there any general characterization you can make that might account for Socrates' way of responding to *aporia* when it occurs in a dialogue? Try to come up with one.

5. Xenophon wrote of Socrates, "He did not approach everybody in the same way" (p. 104). This statement may be interpreted to suggest that Socrates was psychologically astute, or could gauge people's character with great sensitivity. Taking this interpretation as a hypothesis, see if you can understand the four cases where Socrates seems to offer a distinctive response to *aporia* as being responsive to *the particular character of the person* he is talking to and *the particular context of the dialogue* at that moment.

6. In the *Symposium,* as you have read, Alcibiades—after trying to seduce Socrates—wakes up after having slept the night naked under Socrates' tunic to discover that "nothing happened." Could we define this moment as a moment of *aporia?* In what way is it such a moment? In what way is it not such a moment?

7. Let us assume that the story Alcibiades tells at the end of the *Symposium* illustrates Xenophon's sentence, "He did not approach everybody in the same way." Exactly how *did* Socrates approach Alcibiades—and why?

Part II (20 minutes): Class discussion of the results

* * *

Like all conceptual workshops, "*Aporia*" attempts to create a genuine experience for students, one that is engaging, challenging, educational, and whole. How does it aim to produce this outcome? It does so in three ways: (1) It converts a product of knowledge into a process. (2) It provides a whole experience with a beginning, middle, and end. (3) It gets the teacher out of the middle of the classroom configuration.

Converting Products of Knowledge into Processes that Lead to Them

First, the conceptual workshop substitutes an intellectually structured environment for the direct Telling of the teacher. I thought it important for students to understand the concept of *aporia* and see its dynamic role in Socratic dialogue. I wanted them not only to be able to identify moments of *aporia* in the texts, but to grasp how these moments functioned dramatically and psychologically in changing the ongoing conversation.

I could have easily given a lecture on this topic. In fact, I selected this worksheet as a specimen because, just from reading it, you can imagine what the lecture would have looked like. But I did not give a lecture; I converted my lecture into a blueprint for an experience. By means of sequenced, focused problems, I attempted to get students to discover for themselves the conclusions that would have been main tenets of my lecture. I converted my own knowledge back into the processes that led me (or others) to generate that knowledge, making my students generalize from six specific examples and then examine dramatic consequences in four of those cases.

Although the worksheet is organized as a sequence of questions, beneath the separate questions lies one overall *problem-to-be-solved*. This underlying problem provides the *focus* for the intellectual work and the *unity* for the intellectual experience the students will undergo in pursuing their work. In "*Aporia*" the problem-to-be-solved might be formulated as follows:

> In reading many Socratic dialogues, we find that Socrates' questions invariably lead each person he is conversing with to a similar state of psychological confusion, a state of mind that seems to prevent their proceeding further and threatens to abort the inquiry. What are the implications of this repeated pattern for Socrates' manner of pursuing philosophy?

Of course, the worksheet doesn't pose the problem so baldly and pedantically. Rather it leads the student to it by concrete and gradual means. Nevertheless, any reader of the worksheet can see that this problem is guiding its author every step of the way.

In the Canary Problem we can similarly locate a single problem-to-be-solved that serves as its organizing principle:

> What force overcomes the force of gravity when a bird takes flight, allowing the bird to fly in an upward direction, and what evidence is there of that force in a closed physical system?

I decided to teach my students the concept of *aporia* by presenting them a problem-to-be-solved rather than directly explaining the concept to them. But I didn't just give them one problem and let them flounder. I charted a journey for them, and gave them guideposts at each stage. There is an art to finding the right amount of guidance for an intellectual journey. Too much, and the teacher ends up with a lecture posing as "active learning." Too little, and students get lost, become frustrated, and make no discoveries at all. To find the right balance, a teacher has to know her students well, and also her subject matter.

Additionally, there is an art to writing conceptual worksheets that allow students of diverse capacity (and preparation) to engage the questions and get somewhere. The same problem, if well selected and posed appropriately, can provoke different levels of response in different students. Within limits, therefore, different students will have different kinds of learning experiences in response to the same worksheet.

Making the Experience Whole

Second, the conceptual workshop not only converts a product of knowledge into an intellectual experience, it also aims to make that experience "whole." The workshop needs a beginning, a middle, and an end. The first question of "*Aporia*" constitutes the beginning. The beginning of an intellectual experience must provide a ready way for students to engage their minds, using the ideas and knowledge they already bring to it. A concrete problem is usually the best place to begin. In this case, the six quotations provide the concrete starting point. These passages are all taken from dialogues they have read. The material is familiar, but the selections, juxtaposed as they are, also provide something new. For, when originally read, the moments quoted sped by quickly; there was no particular reason (except in the vivid *Meno* passage) for them to stand out. The first question posed, while not overly difficult, is an interesting one; it leads students to see something new in already familiar material.

The beginning will either introduce the problem-to-be-solved that motivates the entire conceptual workshop or it will set the stage for its later presentation. In "*Aporia*" the first question introduces the problem-to-be-solved in a direct and straightforward way. But it doesn't develop the problem fully. That will not happen until the third question.

The second question begins the middle phase of the experience. This is, of course, the most extended phase, and also the most differentiated. It is likely to have several sub-phases, since it provides the "meat" of the experience: the part most responsible for the change in thinking the teacher is hoping for.

In this worksheet, questions 2–5 constitute the middle phase. Question 2 allows the students to refine and clarify their answer to Question 1 by asking how well their explanation of *aporia* fits when applied to an extreme caricature (the paralyzing effects of bedbugs). Question 3 ("Describe what Socrates does in response to each moment of *aporia*") advances the understanding of the concept itself by moving from its *meaning* to its *function*. It sends the students back to their texts and makes them examine the role played by the state of *aporia* in the dramatic forward motion of the Socratic conversations. But to begin with, only specific answers are asked for, a different one for each dialogue. Question 4 then asks for a generalization from the specifics: What is common to all four cases? This turns out to be a difficult question.

Question 5 ("Try to see Socrates' responses as specific to the character of the interlocutor") is useful regardless of whether students have answered question 4 successfully or not. It provides some clues and prompts either a refinement or a revision of the answer to question 4 (*the* central question of the worksheet). By the time they have finished question 5, students should have a pretty good initial understanding of the concept of *aporia*. This understanding will not have been given to them; they will have built it on their own as a group.

An intellectual ending to the experience is provided by questions 6 and 7. In a way analogous to question 5 of the Canary Problem, questions 6 and 7 together ask students to apply their new understanding to a situation both similar to and different from the cases from which they have developed that understanding (here, a rather bizarre case—Alcibiades' failed seduction of Socrates). This demand forces them to test their new ideas, to sharpen the edges of their conception of *aporia,* to convert what may still be a rough and rigid framework to one that is more dynamic and flexible. It provokes crystallization of the concept as well, so that when the experience is over they have something to take away from it. (New ideas, even when clear for a moment, have a way of falling apart when one turns attention elsewhere.)

But, as discussed above, an intellectual ending is not sufficient; an ending that provides social, emotional, *and* intellectual satisfaction is best. So, for the reasons specified in our discussion of the Canary Problem, the worksheet offers a Part II in which the whole class comes together and, under the teacher's guidance, discusses both their answers to the worksheet questions and their experiences struggling to come up with those answers.

Reconfiguring the Classroom: Getting the Teacher Out of the Middle

Third, after the teacher has created an intellectual experience for her students and made it whole, she restructures the physical and emotional configuration of the classroom. The typical classroom is organized around a teacher. Physically, she is usually at the front of the class, facing a group of students, all of whom are facing her (and ignoring each other). Emotionally, she occupies the center of the class, the chief object of each student's concern. She is like the hub of a wheel, and each student is like a small segment of the wheel's rim. The spokes of the wheel vividly designate the axes of attention and concern in the traditional classroom.

But in a conceptual workshop, the teacher steps out of the middle. Instead of mediating between the students and the material, she places the students in direct contact with the material, stepping to one side to permit a direct encounter. The class now looks like a series of small wheels: Students still constitute the rims, but now the intellectual material is at the hub. The teacher is reduced to acting as a mechanic who roves around making sure the wheels turn smoothly.

This reconfiguration of the classroom depends importantly on one simple fact: The questions and instructions have been written out ahead of time, reproduced, and distributed to each student. If the teacher transmits her questions orally or at the board, then she is back to having all eyes and ears on her. And the moment confusion arises, the students are forced to deal with her personally. With a written worksheet, the teacher's instructions are still present, but depersonalized. The students don't have to turn away from their classmates toward the teacher to recall the instructions; they can simply scrutinize the worksheet they have at hand and no disruption of the small group becomes necessary.

The new classroom configuration of the conceptual workshop yields three distinctive virtues. The first is that it takes the students' attention off the teacher and places it directly on the material. The second is that it allows the teacher to exploit the learning potential of the group. Most teachers abstractly recognize the value of class discussion in promoting learning. But in traditional classrooms, discussions aren't usually spontaneous or genuine, and they don't get very far. Typically, interchanges between the teacher and individual students pass for "class discussion," and if spontaneous debate or thoughtful inquiry does break out among students, it is usually short-lived. Or, a teacher may throw out a "discussion question" to her class, and suffer painfully along with her students while everyone waits for "discussion" to ensue. If it does at all, the discussion take place among the two or three students who everyone knows can be counted on to carry the ball and satisfy the teacher. Neither of these familiar situations produces the kind of discussions teachers hope for when they decide to take a step away from Telling and toward generating a more electric classroom environment.

But the conceptual workshop avoids these pitfalls. If, at the worst, only two students carry the ball in a discussion group of four, then you've got half the class talking right there. And students can't direct their responses to the teacher in the course of the workshop, because she is not there; she is off somewhere else listening in on another group. And so, if the questions are well written—if they are clearly focused, build on each other, and allow the students to make intellectual progress—students find they can learn a lot through discussion. Almost all the benefits of "letting the students do the talking" discussed in Chapter 3 come into play during conceptual workshops, but in an environment where the shape and direction of the conversation have been dictated by the teacher. The group nature of the work contributes a social texture to the experience that makes a big emotional difference. Students leave successful conceptual workshops feeling they have really accomplished something, and the emphasis is not only on "accomplished" but also on "they."

The third virtue of the reconfigured classroom is the unparalleled opportunity it offers the teacher for witnessing the level of understanding that her students bring to the subject matter she is teaching. During all the time she is sitting in on the small discussion groups, she is hearing her students' responses to her specific, pointed questions about the material. When a small number of students discuss specific concepts and concrete examples in detail, their level of understanding is dramatically revealed to an educated listener. Their implicit assumptions, the gaps in their knowledge, the way they connect ideas together, what they distinguish and what they fail to distinguish—all this and more becomes evident to an attentive teacher.

Listening to these discussions is inevitably a humbling experience. It almost always shows that students are less far along than the teacher has assumed. It usually reveals a need to back up a few steps and go over (by whatever means) material that the teacher assumed the students had mastered. For obvious reasons, many teachers would prefer to be spared exposure to this evidence. But if they take their intellectual goals seriously, and if their goals pertain to what the students are *learning,* and not simply to what they themselves are *teaching,* then they will be grateful for this insider's view of their students' understanding. It will show them, better than any classroom discussion or exam, what they need to do next to make progress toward the understanding they are after.

Putting the Students to Work

Imagine for a moment that you are the teacher of a college course on Shakespeare. You have forty students in your class and you meet them for two-hour sessions. The next play on the syllabus is *Troilus and Cressida,* one of the most perplexing and problematic of Shakespeare's plays. It presents a nasty world peopled with petty characters; critics have never even agreed whether to call it a comedy or a tragedy—clearly it is neither. It has puzzled readers and audiences ever since it was written.

But you have a bright idea about how to approach it. Your idea is to consider the play as part of a sequence of plays: *Henry V, Julius Caesar, Hamlet,* and *Troilus and Cressida* (and they were almost certainly written in this order, although with other plays intervening). Once these four plays are viewed as a series, certain themes emerge, and *Troilus,* extreme as it is, begins to make sense, since it presents the end point of a progression (or regression).

Your first thought is to write a brilliant lecture developing your ideas. But then you ask yourself: "Why not make the students do the intellectual work they would normally watch me perform in a lecture?" It would be easy enough, in this case, to design a conceptual workshop to this end. All you have to do is to present them with your central hypothesis and ask them to investigate each of the themes that you think are germane. The worksheet couldn't be simpler.

First you present your hypothesis: "Consider *Troilus and Cressida* to be the final play in a sequence of four," going on to name the other three in the appropriate order. Then, in Part I, you present six themes (e.g., "the balance struck between honor and self-interest"; "the kind of world the characters inhabit"; "the nature of the father (or father figures)"; "the shape and function of anger"). You ask your students to trace each theme, one at a time, through each of the four plays in order, instructing them to spend ten minutes discussing each theme and to take notes on their discussions. In Part II, you ask them to synthesize the results of their six small discussions by answering in writing one general question about the major theme you think connects all four plays ("the challenge to a young man of achieving a viable adult male identity"). Part III is devoted to hearing and discussing each group's answer to that question. (The worksheet is included in the Appendix to this chapter.)

It is the evening before the class and you have written your worksheet. You suddenly realize that nothing prevents you from still giving your brilliant lecture—*after* your students have done the conceptual workshop! What could better prepare them to learn from your lecture than the experience of having done this workshop? And what could interest them more in your lecture? Not only will they listen with fascination, but they will now be in a position to critically appraise your ideas, since they will have "researched" the same topics and developed their own point of view on the material.

If you have never designed and conducted a conceptual workshop before, there is a further aspect of the experience you will not appreciate until the next day when the workshop actually takes place: what it feels like to be a teacher in the midst of a class run as a conceptual workshop. Let us assume for simplicity's sake that your students are familiar with conceptual workshops and have participated in them many times before, but this is your first experience "running" one.

You pass out the worksheets and tell the students to get started. There is a brief pause as they read the initial instructions telling them what size groups to form, then some scuffling and shuffling, and before you know it, small groups have appeared all over the room, and students are busy at work. All eyes face inward, and the groups begin to talk quietly. The sounds of the many groups blend together, creating a busy and surprisingly soothing hum. No one is looking at you. In fact, there appears to be nothing for you to do! You feel strangely uncomfortable, the odd man out. What kind of a class is this, you find yourself wondering, where there is no comfortable position for a teacher to occupy?

So you leave to get a cup of coffee. Five minutes later, coffee in hand, you quietly open the door to the classroom, half-convinced it will be empty. But lo, the students are all there working away; no one seems to have noticed either your exit or your subsequent entrance. And now your mood shifts. Forty students are working hard, and you don't have to do anything but sip coffee! "What a great job," you think, forgetting the many hours you spent, first studying the plays and then designing the worksheet. You feel a great load lift from your shoulders. The class is running itself, and you are free to watch, listen, put in your two cents where you think it might help, and simply oil the gears of this industrious "workshop" of busy workers. (You feel the full impact of the term for the first time.) And so you go over to one group of students, pull up a chair, and begin to listen. And then things begin to get really interesting.

Creating Blueprints for Learning

In a way, designing experiences that teach (via conceptual workshops) is one instance of "teaching through writing" (discussed in Chapter 5). The teacher writes a document and gives it to her students. The document is a blueprint for an experience. By following the instructions on the document, by working together to solve the problems she has set for them, the students will have an intellectual experience. From the experience, if things go well, they will learn. (For another example of a conceptual workshop, see the Appendix Follow-Up to Chapter 9.)

Writing is thus the primary medium through which the teacher does her teaching. The main differences between this approach to teaching through writing and those discussed in the previous chapter are (1) the teacher's presence is still required—*some* talking will be needed to supplement the writing, and (2) the teacher's writing doesn't tell or explain; it poses problems and sets forth activities. The conceptual workshop is thus an instance of teaching even further removed from Telling than the cases of teaching through writing discussed in Chapter 5.

Though the teacher refuses to directly Tell her students what she thinks about the subject matter, she is not withholding her knowledge from them. A glance at any decent conceptual worksheet will show just how much she is giving them. Designing a specific intellectual experience rests on a foundation of knowledge. A teacher needs three kinds of knowledge to succeed: (1) knowledge of the subject matter, (2) knowledge of how a grasp of that subject matter is best put together (i.e., of how the subject matter is best learned), and (3) an overall knowledge of the strengths and weaknesses of her students.

The teacher, then, attempts to create a blueprint for learning by keeping her mouth shut and instead designing an environment for her students with the following three features: (1) The teacher presents an overall problem-to-be-solved, which is broken down into smaller problems that build on each other and which requires an advance in thinking to solve. The teacher thus converts her own knowledge back into intellectual activities and induces her students to go through these activities for themselves. (2) The teacher creates a blueprint for a "whole" experience; she provides a beginning, a middle, and an end. (3) She reconfigures the classroom so that she is "out of the middle" so the students can focus their attention on: (a) the subject matter, (b) each other, and (c) the written questions and instructions she has distributed to each of them. By creating such an environment, she is giving her students a great deal. She is Teaching them. Yet her mouth remains closed.

Appendix to Chapter 6
The Canary Problem

1. A canary is standing on the bottom of a very large sealed bottle that is placed on a scale. The bird takes off and flies around the inside of the bottle. What happens to the reading of the scale? Explain.

2. A goldfish is lying on the bottom of a large goldfish bowl filled with water that is placed on a scale. The fish takes off and swims around the inside of the bowl. What happens to the reading of the scale? Explain.

3. A man is standing on a scale. He then gets off the scale, places a large metal spiral spring (as large as he is) on the scale, and stands on top of the spring. What happens to the reading of the scale? Explain. (For simplicity's sake, ignore the weight of the spring itself in answering this question.)

4. Suppose the man above replaces the spring on the scale by an "air-spring." This is a cylinder (as large as the man) with a piston that slides down into it. There is a column of air trapped in the cylinder, and the man stands on a platform mounted atop the piston. The cylinder is open at the bottom, but is connected to the scale by an air-tight seal. Compare the scale readings when the man is on the air-spring as opposed to when he is directly on the scale. Explain. (Once again, ignore the weight of the air-spring itself.)

5. (a) In the canary problem in 1, suppose the bottle is replaced by a cage that is mostly glass, but with very thin spaces between the glass bars. What happens?

   (b) Suppose it is replaced by an ordinary wire cage?

   (c) Suppose the bird is hovering over the scale and is not enclosed at all?

   (d) What if the bird simply flies over the scale?

Discuss.

Shakespeare's Truth
Spring 1999

WORKSHOP: From *Henry V* to *Troilus and Cressida*

Divide into groups of four.

Introduction: The purpose of this workshop is to situate *Troilus and Cressida* at the end of a sequence of four plays (*Henry V, Julius Caesar, Hamlet, Troilus and Cressida*—written in that order) to trace Shakespeare's developing treatment of a number of interrelated issues. This kind of analysis provides excellent preparation for formulating an interpretation of the play. I will include in the Program Notebook in the library a paper that presents the interpretation I arrived at after doing work of a kind similar to that required by this workshop.

Part I (60 minutes):

For each of the subjects below, trace through the sequence of four plays and discuss how each play treats or presents the subject in question. Take notes on the highlights of your discussions. Spend about ten minutes on each.

1. the balance struck between honor and self-interest;
2. the kind of world the characters inhabit;
3. the image of women (as "love objects");
4. the nature of the father (or "father figures");
5. the image of brotherhood;
6. the shape and function of anger.

Part II (30 minutes):

Synthesize the results of your analyses from Part I by first discussing, and then writing an answer to, the following questions: How does each play envisage and treat the challenge of growing from boyhood to manhood and of achieving a viable identity as man/king/husband/future-father? In addition, what shape is there to the *progression* of Shakespeare's treatments of these themes over the four plays?

Part III (30 minutes)

Meet together as a whole class to discuss your responses to Part II.

7

Refusing To "Teach"
Separating Power and Authority in the Classroom

Becoming Self-Conscious about Power and Authority

In earlier discussions I mentioned the special attention students pay to their teacher because of his power and authority. In this chapter, I will distinguish between power and authority, and show how a teacher can turn his awareness of this difference into a powerful educational instrument. Becoming self-conscious about power and authority in the classroom means becoming "political" in the broadest sense; a teacher who makes this move must also be willing to refuse to give his students what they most want from him.

"I Am Not Going to Tell You What to Do"

Imagine yourself in the following situation. You have enrolled in a college course on Shakespeare. The class meets four days a week (Monday through Thursday) for two hours a session. On the first day of class the teacher, Dr. Ford, explains the weekly schedule. Each week the class will read one play. There will be two open-ended seminars (see Chapter 3) each week to discuss the play, one on Monday and one on Thursday. The other two classes will be teacher-directed: on Tuesday, a conceptual workshop (see Chapter 6) introducing techniques of literary analysis, or sometimes a film or a lecture; on Wednesday, a writing lab in which drafts of students' essays will be scrutinized and critiqued.

Dr. Ford explains that Tuesdays and Wednesdays are his days to set the agenda, direct the students' thinking, and lead the class. On Mondays and Thursdays, by contrast, the students will set their own agenda, direct their

111

own thinking, and lead themselves as they try to make sense of a particular play. He then passes out the syllabus, goes over the remaining logistics of the course, assigns the first play (*Romeo and Juliet,* due the next day) and concludes by saying, "I'll see you in seminar tomorrow."

The next day you enter the seminar room to find an oval table with chairs around it. Dr. Ford is already seated in one of them about two-thirds of the way along the long side of the oval. He has his Shakespeare text open, a pad of paper next to it, and his attention appears to be totally absorbed in the pages of his book. Occasionally, he scribbles some words on his pad. Other students hesitantly walk in, look around the room, and slowly take seats, the first ones as far away from the professor as possible, the last ones forced to sit near and finally next to him. The bell rings to signal the start of the period.

Everyone waits for Dr. Ford to look up and say something. But he does no such thing. For two or three minutes he continues to read and scribble. Then he looks up, gazes around the room, but says nothing. The silence in the room builds. Already it has become terribly uncomfortable, and the seconds ticking by seem like hours.

Finally, four minutes into the class (but it seems like a half-hour), Dr. Ford speaks: "You appear to think that I didn't mean what I said yesterday. But I did. This class is a seminar. It is up to you decide how to use the two hours we have. The only rule is that we are here to discuss the play assigned for the week. But it's up to you to decide what's worth talking about, and how to talk about it. I am not going to tell you what to do. I will listen to what you say; I expect to learn from your discussion. If I learn something important by listening to your discussion, I will tell it to you. Occasionally, if I think I can help you at a particular moment, I will say something. But don't expect me to say much. I have Tuesday and Wednesday each week to do my teaching in. These seminars on Monday and Thursday are yours. So you might as well get started."

He then ceases to talk. Once again the silence starts to build. Everybody's eyes are on Dr. Ford. He meets their gaze, seems perfectly relaxed, and waits. Another unbearable minute goes by. Finally, one brave soul stammers, "Uh, . . . *Romeo and Juliet* was so sad. But, their parents . . . they made me so mad. Why should the kids pay the price because the parents were so stubborn?"

More silence, but then more quickly, another student: "Mercutio was so cool. His jokes were great. I wish Shakespeare hadn't killed him off so soon."

Another pause, this time a long one. A third student: "Did Shakespeare believe in God? I couldn't figure out the religious point of view in this play."

And then finally a connected response from yet another student: "What's God got to do with this play?"

The conversation limps along. Everyone keeps looking at the professor, convinced that surely by now he will step in and rescue everyone from the disaster that is only getting worse by the minute. But he shows no signs of doing anything; he doesn't even appear bothered by what is happening. The clock on the wall shows that only fifteen minutes have elapsed since the bell rang, though the clock must be broken, since surely it has been at least an hour. But no, the clock is not broken, and yes, you're going to have sit there for another hour and three-quarters!

What Happens When a Teacher Refuses to "Teach"?

What happens when a teacher refuses to tell his students what to do in class? The reader might first wish to ask: *Why* would a teacher refuse to tell his students what to do in class? But I will defer that question until I address the first one. What happens when a teacher refuses to "teach"?

The above description gives a pretty good picture of how such a class is likely to begin on its first day. But the class cannot stay that horrible for long. Fairly soon, it dawns on the students that the teacher means what he says. They then begin to use their time to try to discuss the play at hand. How they actually go about this task will depend on the particular group. Some may adopt some standard routines for beginning, some may assign a special role to specific students, perhaps rotating the role of "facilitator," or asking a different student each week to do some extra research and start the class off with a brief report. But most will simply use the allotted time to do their best in discussing the play without trying to structure the time in advance.

With any luck, three weeks later, the class that started by agonizing over their teacher's silence will launch happily into a discussion when the bell rings, proud of their newfound ability to discuss a work of literature in their teacher's presence without his direct assistance.

But let us look more closely at this "independent" group of students having a seminar. Let us now imagine ourselves, not as participants sharing in the emotions of the group, as we did previously, but as silent observers, sitting against the wall, ignored by the group, watching as carefully as we can all that happens.

The first things we notice confirm our initial impression. The students have come prepared—most of them—to talk about the play. Some have questions, and most seem thoroughly familiar with the details of the play. They listen to each other, and they try to respond to each other. They refer to specific events in the play to back up their statements, and sometimes they flip through the pages of their book to find a passage, which they read aloud.

These details strike us immediately. But after a few minutes another dimension of the discussion begins to dawn on us. When a student speaks, even in direct response to another student, she looks, not at the person she is addressing, but at Dr. Ford, sitting silently in his seat. Despite the unresponsive manner he maintains, this pattern repeats itself over and over. Occasionally, he scribbles something on his pad right after a student has spoken. This action seems to make the student terribly anxious. Dr. Ford cannot look up from his pad, lean forward, or raise his eyebrow without its being noticed by virtually everyone in the class. No one mentions any of these actions, but it is clear from the students' expressions that nothing he does goes unnoticed.

Occasionally, as he said he would, Dr. Ford speaks. The class goes dead quiet the minute he takes in a breath of air in anticipation of speaking. The level of attentiveness is ten times higher than when any student speaks. Even though he speaks quickly, and not too loudly, not a word of what he says is missed. Though the students have notebooks open in front of them, they rarely write much down. However, the teacher's words are the exception. When he speaks, suddenly pens are in motion, pages rustle, ink is spent. Ironically, this writing is probably unnecessary since it turns out that everyone can remember every word Dr. Ford has uttered in class, without the aid of any notes.

By withholding his words, by refusing to lead, by making himself a near-silent observer of the group, the teacher has magnified his own importance in the class in a strange way. The less he says, the more each word counts. The more he acts in accordance with the dictum that the class belongs to the students, the more the class looks like a performance staged just for him. What kind of a classroom has he created?

Why Would a Teacher Refuse to "Teach"?

First, let us look at the teacher's motives. Why does he refuse to lead his class? He has reasons at three levels. At the first level, his reasons are the ones he told his students. He thinks it important that they have a place to discuss their own questions about the book, and he wants them to be able to make their own discoveries (individually and as a group).

At the second level, he wants them to develop a capacity to inquire as a group without relying on his authority. He wants them to develop independence of mind, autonomy of thought. He wants them to discover that they *can* make discoveries on their own, and so boost their own confidence in their intellectual powers.

The third level is the most complex. To some degree, the aims described under the first two levels could be met by work done in out-of-class study groups with no teacher present (see Chapter 3). The crucial factor in the scene we are examining is that *the teacher is present but refuses to direct the class.* Thus the students have to take over his functions right in front of his face. Or, they have to willfully refuse to take over his functions right in front him. Either way, the teacher's power becomes an issue for the class; it becomes part of what the class is about, whatever else is under discussion. Dr. Ford considers this consequence a virtue. He sees it as a way of helping the students to grow up, not just emotionally, but intellectually—he doesn't really separate these two dimensions.

He doesn't really separate the three levels we have distinguished, either. He considers that students cannot go far in learning Shakespeare (or any subject) without (a) learning how to respond to the plays on their own terms, (b) learning how to *sustain* inquiry so they get beyond their initial responses to a text, and (c) learning how to develop an authoritative voice of their own in talking about Shakespeare, overcoming their inherent awe of the teacher's authority. These three objectives require that he leave the burden of inquiry on their shoulders, that he let them struggle without helping them too much, and that he force them to struggle in front of him. He may help occasionally, but not so much that the students come to believe that he will take over when the going gets too hard, or when they signal him that they simply don't feel like struggling any longer. In sum, *the teacher refuses to govern the students in their inquiry because he wants the students to learn how to govern themselves.*

Democracy in Education

Thus, without advertising the fact, Dr. Ford has created a *political* classroom. This is the answer to the question: "What kind of a classroom has he created?" He wants his students to learn to govern themselves—he has a political aim, a *democratic* aim. Why would a teacher of Shakespeare hold this aim?

Three reasons might move such a teacher. First, inquiry itself is inherently democratic. In Chapter 3, by examining the debater's paradox in the *Meno,* we saw that inquiry demands relinquishing faith in Authority to deliver the truth. *Individual* inquiry requires a trust that one's own intellectual powers can yield sound conclusions. *Collective* inquiry requires of the individual that same trust in the group's capacity for inquiry, a group of which he is a part. This trust is inherently democratic. As many have pointed out, the international community of scientists may present the best example we have of an international democratic community. Whatever its flaws and strains, this self-governing community is founded on mutual respect and a faith in no authority other than that of the human mind. A teacher who wishes to train independent thinkers, then, will be committed to fostering democratic aims in his classroom. In promoting collective inquiry, he is already promoting democracy.

The second reason is more straightforward; he may simply wish to promote democracy through his teaching. He may be "political" in the everyday sense of the term and believe it his duty to teach future citizens to participate effectively in a democratic society.

But he need not be "political" in this direct sense to hold the aim of promoting democracy through teaching. He may rather believe that his duty as a teacher is to promote *the development of the character of his students* (the third reason). He may think his vocation requires him to do all he can to promote his students' independence of mind, self-reliance, autonomy, judgment, sense of responsibility, and capacity to work productively as members of a group. But these character traits are just what is needed for democratic participation. Developing them is the very aim a "political" teacher will hold if his aim is democracy. Thus, a teacher may create a "democratic classroom" without considering himself "political" at all. He will do so as a means to stimulate the character development of his students toward an ideal of maturity he considers an end in itself.

Let the Classroom Environment Do the Talking

Another way to teach with your mouth shut, then, is to create a classroom environment that both invites and promotes democratic participation. A teacher who takes this path is likely to distinguish between two different teaching aims. In addition to wanting his students to learn his subject, he will try to develop in them a certain kind of character.

The more ambitious aim of character development makes the limitations of teaching through Telling more glaring. Simply telling children to be responsible, to think for themselves, to be dependable (and in general to have such-and-such kind of character) is, for the most part, an exercise in futility. If we could develop character in a child by simply ordering up the desired type, a parent's job would be a thousand times easier than it is. Character development is just not that simple.

Character develops in response to an environment. The immediate environment in which we operate has a structure: It presents constraints, demands, orientations, limits, opportunities, and invitations. Adaptive creatures that we are, we respond directly to the press of our environment, and over time, we are shaped by how we respond. (This is only half the story; we shape our environment, too.) Habitual responses become habits, dispositions to respond in certain ways. The stable organization of these dispositions is what we call "character."

Speech is part of our environment, so what we are told cannot be ignored when assessing our environment's structure. But speech is one of the least powerful aspects of our surroundings; a locked door is harder to argue with than a command to "stay in your room." Setting up a swing set in the backyard is more persuasive than repeatedly urging a child to "go outside and get some exercise." So, *for some purposes,* locking the door or building a swing set is a more effective way to design an environment than talking.

Those who would try to shape the character of developing humans are likely to succeed best by structuring the environment of their charges and keeping their own mouths shut. Let the environment do the talking! A favorite trick of seasoned pre-school teachers is to position a table in a space where children are likely to run. Once the table is in place, the need to constantly urge youngsters not to run vanishes. In a similar vein, high school teachers who wish to stimulate active discussion do well to rearrange their students' chairs into a circle, to leave the front of the class, and to occupy one of those chairs.

These simple examples are designed more to influence behavior than shape character. In this chapter, we are discussing a greater challenge: shaping the student's character toward one that will be competent to participate in a democratic community (especially a democratic community of inquiry). And we are examining the possibility of using a classroom that requires democratic participation as a means to that end.

But this description is too broad. We can imagine a teacher who holds the above aim designing a classroom far different from Dr. Ford's: one with rules for participation (e.g., Robert's Rules of Order), strict procedures for making decisions, and a list of narrow objectives all laid out in advance according to a timetable. A rationale based on the need to learn the prerequisite skills for democratic participation through clear instruction and repeated practice would probably lie behind this tight organization. Designing such a classroom is one way for a teacher to try to shape character through creating a democratic classroom, but it is not the way I will discuss in this chapter.

We began by examining a classroom that was almost the exact opposite of the one just envisaged. In that classroom, Dr. Ford organized an environment for his students by giving them: (1) one limit (they were there to discuss a play), (2) one central constraint ("I will not tell you what to do"), (3) a general but vague orientation ("you will have to figure out what to talk about and how to talk about it"), (4) a minimal promise of support ("If I think I can help you, I will say something, but don't expect me to say much"), and (5) a sense of the seriousness of their task ("I will listen to what you say; I expect to learn from your discussion").

Then he left them on their own to flounder and struggle. Dr. Ford showed his willingness to watch this struggle for unlimited amounts of time. He also showed his ability to avoid being seduced into taking over the reins of the class in the face of dismal results, boring stretches of flat discussion, and student appeals of all sorts. Dr. Ford "teaches" democracy as if he believes in the advice given by one writer on the subject: "the only real education system for democracy *is* democracy" (emphasis added). He seems to think that because the environment in which he has placed his students requires democratic participation for it to flourish, the students will eventually find their way to participating democratically. And so he keeps his mouth shut and waits for the environment to do its work.

Do Not Confuse the Product with the Instrument

But there appears to be a problem here. Recall what we found when we imagined ourselves against the wall observing the third week of class. Rather than a class of equals participating together independently and interdependently, we discovered a collection of dependent students whose sole aim seemed to be to win the approval of their teacher. Each speaker cared more about Dr. Ford's reaction to her comment than the reactions of the other students. We observed a group of students strangely ruled by a silent teacher, whose few words and gestures were taken as oracular. Dr. Ford seems to have brought forth the very opposite of a democratically functioning community of inquiry.

To get some perspective on this problem, let us again consult Jean-Jacques Rousseau (from his book *Emile, or On Education,* published in 1762).

> The masterpiece of a good education is to make a reasonable man, and they [traditional tutors] claim they raise a child by reason! This is to begin with the end, to want to make the product the instrument.

Rousseau's point is that if a child has not reached an age where he has developed the capacity for reason, then you will not make him reasonable by appealing to his reason, that is, by appealing to a capacity he does not yet have. To act in this way is to confuse an end of development with the means for reaching that end ("to make the product the instrument").

Instead, Rousseau argues, you must observe your child, consider the capacities that he actually possesses at any given age, and then treat him in a manner that both (a) takes those capacities into account, and (b) paves the way for the capacity you wish to foster. "Paving the way" means creating the necessary foundations, and it also means *not* creating obstacles that will *prevent* the development of the capacity you desire. Repeatedly giving a child incapable of understanding them a long list of reasons for a simple prohibition is more likely to stimulate in him a distaste for rational argument than to lead to its development. Such a distaste is one of the obstacles Rousseau wishes to avoid. ("With each lesson that one wants to put into their heads before its proper time, a vice is planted in the depth of their hearts.")

And so, Rousseau demands that the teacher combine a profound understanding of his student with a profound understanding of the capacity he is trying to foster (reason, in this example). This two-fold understanding will allow him to design an environment in which his student can "run free," yet which will "silently" promote the development the teacher considers to be in the student's best interest. The student's free interaction with that environment—his bumping into its limits, demands, opportunities, and invitations—will both sharpen the prior capacities on which the desired capacity depends and avoid creating "vices" in his heart that will block healthy development. He will thus become reasonable (when the time for reason arrives) without any imposition of reason on him along the way.

And so with our "democratic classroom," we must not confuse the product with the instrument. We must not be deceived into thinking that Dr. Ford has really created a democratically functioning classroom by setting up the environment he has. Though at first it may appear otherwise, he is not confusing the end with the means; he does not think he can bring about democracy by fiat. His seeming belief that "the only education system for democracy is democracy" is a misleading appearance. What he has created in his classroom is not democracy but a set of conditions that he hopes will "pave the way" to democracy. He knows that his students are not yet capable of democratic participation, just as Rousseau's young child was not capable of mature reason. He wants to develop in them capacities for democracy, and he knows that this development is slow and imperfect.

Transference

The crucial step in this development is the students' becoming aware of their own yearning for dependence. To be capable of governing themselves, people must first become acquainted with their desire to be governed, to be taken care of by a superior being. This desire is virtually universal and usually unconscious. That we all harbor this deep yearning was one of Freud's great discoveries (one of the few that is likely to survive the current falling into disfavor of most of his thought).

Freud's insights into human psychology were grounded in his profound appreciation of how utterly helpless and dependent human infants are, and how long, slow, and painful the development out of dependency is for human children. As infants, our very survival depends on our parents and their ability to fulfill our fundamental needs for food, warmth, security, and love. Deprived of these fundamentals, we scream in terror. When Mommy arrives at the sound of our scream, picks us up, nestles us to her breast, and satisfies all our needs at once with milk, physical warmth, caresses, billing, comfort, and love, we are in bliss. What could be more satisfying than having all one's physical needs met simultaneously by an all-knowing, all-powerful creature who seems to know our every need and how to meet it perfectly? We never forget these moments. We carry them in our body, in our cells, in the deepest layers of our mind (in our "unconscious," Freud would say).

Gradually we learn to separate from this marvelous creature, and to put up with our needs, even when they are not instantly met. Gradually we develop more complex needs that could not possibly be met so easily and quickly by any single human being, no matter how much she loved us.

But we never forget. And we can never completely give up the yearning attached to those deep memories of complete fulfillment. We yearn for an all-powerful being who will make everything all right, who will take care of us, who will take care of things for us. At our weakest moments—when we are exhausted or at the end of our rope—we may become aware of this wish. Maturity is, in part, measured not so much by our ability to give up this yearning as by our ability not to base our actions and decisions on it. We accept, finally, that we must look after ourselves, and that even those who love us will never be able to satisfy us completely. And we try to live our lives according to this hard knowledge. But still, at moments, how we wish it were otherwise! And at our weakest moments, some of us have been known to make decisions forgetting that it is not otherwise.

Freud made these discoveries by noticing that patients in psychoanalysis developed unrealistically powerful feelings of both love and hate toward their psychoanalysts, as well as strong fantasies about them. He realized that these feelings and fantasies had their origins in the patient's relation to a parent or parental figure in early childhood, and that the patient had *transferred* from the parent to the analyst these strong, unconscious patterns of feeling. He therefore called this phenomenon "transference." Subsequent investigations showed how common transference reactions are, not just in psychoanalysis or psychotherapy, but in any two-person relationship where one person has clear power and authority over the other. Similar patterns of feeling can apply to employee and employer, patient and physician, client and attorney, defendant and judge, citizen and political leader, and without question, student and teacher.

Psychoanalysts understand that these transference reactions are so deeply rooted that they cannot be undone. The most to be hoped for is that patients become aware of them and thus learn not to base actions and decisions on them. (They will still yearn, but they will not act as if these yearnings could be realized.) In the same vein, Dr. Ford does not expect his students to stop caring about his approval. He just hopes that they can become aware of their need to be "loved" and "taken care of" by him, and so conduct themselves accordingly.

In order to become a democratic group, students have almost willfully to wrest their attention away from the teacher and turn it toward each other. To make this shift requires becoming aware that their attention is so narrowly focused on the teacher. That is why the teacher's power must become an issue for the class. Any pretense promoted by the teacher that he is no different from any one else in the class only keeps him at the center. What is needed is just the reverse: a palpable demonstration to all that the students regard their teacher as all-powerful—*even though he is refusing to exercise any power at all.*

Power versus Authority

So far in this chapter, I have followed everyday usage in not distinguishing between power and authority. But the two terms have different meanings, and to understand the dynamics of Dr. Ford's class, the distinction is crucial. *Power* is simply the ability to make things happen. Teachers traditionally exercise power by giving assignments, issuing directions, telling students what to do, and of course, by giving grades and awarding or withholding credit.

Authority is quite different. Authority is that which justifies or makes legitimate a particular arrangement or set of affairs. The government of the United States rests on the authority of the Constitution and those who interpret it, the Supreme Court. But notice that neither of these authorities has any power to make anything happen. The Constitution is just a piece of paper. And the Supreme Court has no power of its own; to enforce its decisions it relies on another branch of government (the Executive), which does have power. Authority is something that is appealed to. It is typically grounded in the past or in some transcendent realm (e.g., Heaven). It comes from "beyond." Power, on the other hand, is grounded in present realities (guns or grades, for example).

But there is a good reason why we confuse the two, or to be precise, *fuse* the two in our thinking. In most of our experience, power and authority are joined seamlessly in the same person or institution. They were fused historically, too. When people believed in the divine right of kings to rule, the monarch was the source of both the state's authority and its power. The king's person was linked to heaven and his will legitimized the state; at the same time, he directed the powers of the state. He was judge, legislator, and executive all at once. The genius of modern democratic (or "republican") government is that it distinguishes between and forcibly separates power and authority in the institutions of government.

The idea behind our government is that *the people* have the power; they exercise their power through representatives and so govern themselves. But the people are not sources of authority. In our government, as I said, authority derives from the Constitution (and the hypothesized intentions of those who wrote the Constitution).

Authority thus creates the "circumstances" in which power can be exercised. It allows "the people" to exercise power to govern themselves by providing a stable framework and a *modus operandi* for them to do so. And when there is conflict, as there always will be, our authoritative documents and institutions give us something to appeal to in order to resolve the conflict.

From our childhood, as in history, we can remember a time when power and authority were fused. When we were young, our parents embodied both for us. They were the source of all power in our world. They made things happen for us; we had to appeal to them to get much of what we wanted. At the same time, they were our source of legitimacy. Their words explained the world, and their judgments were final. "Because I say so" is the clearest possible signal that the person speaking is a source of authority. Our parents were transcendent to us, connected to the past, and perhaps also to God.

Since each of us emerged into consciousness from a set of circumstances in which "the divine right of parents" was a felt reality, we have trouble untangling the concepts of power and authority and distinguishing between them. This difficulty is not just a theoretical one; it has the most practical consequences.

To be free to govern ourselves, to set up a democratic community (on a large or small scale), we must be able to take power into our own hands. But at the same time *we must respect the institutions of authority that create the arena in which we aim to exercise power.* The reason why so many revolutions fail, be they political or personal, is that those who would be free, in defeating those who hold power over them, tend also to destroy the sources of authority they need. Successful at seizing power, the rebels then try to exercise it in an authority-vacuum. This situation only paves the way for a new despotism. (Recall that the victors of our own revolution wanted to make George Washington a king to rule over them.)

Separating Power and Authority in the Classroom

What Dr. Ford has done, in a rough and ready way, is to hand over the power of his classroom to his students, while maintaining his authority as their teacher. Let us consider each of these conditions in turn.

First, let's be clear: He has not handed over all his power. He still will be issuing credit and grades, and he still will enforce some minimal rules on the class (they must talk about the play and maintain a certain degree of order and civility).

Regarding the teacher's power, we must make another distinction. A teacher typically has two sources of power, though they are not generally distinguished. First, he is the agent of his institution (the school), and if it is a public school, then also of the state. Second, he is an adult, usually older than his students and inevitably more experienced in matters germane to the course. It is natural for him to assume leadership in such a situation and for others to obey him.

It is hard to distinguish these two aspects of a teacher's power, the institutional and the personal, since we so naturally think of obedience as following the power to punish (e.g., to give grades), a power that for adults is usually rooted in social institutions. But imagine an adult education class where no grades are given. Such classes are typically run in the same manner as regular classes: The teacher tells the students what to do and the students do what the teacher tells them. Students in these classes are no less obedient for the absence of grades. The teacher's personal power suffices.

Dr. Ford has not given up his institutional power. There is no way he can do so and retain his job. He is employed by his college and he is required to give grades. True, he can devise artificial means to get around this requirement, temporary expedients that may work in the short run (such as giving all A's, or letting students grade themselves). But without pursuing that possibility, let us recognize that a teacher can hand over the power to determine *what goes on in the classroom* without handing over his power over *what happens in the course as a whole.*

Indeed, Dr. Ford has been clear about this distinction from the start, saying that he will control what happens on Tuesdays and Wednesdays but not on Mondays and Thursdays. He can also retain his power to give grades in a meaningful way, without maintaining power over what happens in the seminar discussions, as long as he doesn't make the grades dependent on what goes on in those seminars. If he bases his grades exclusively or primarily on exams and essays, and minimally or not at all on seminar participation, then he can meaningfully give up the power over those classes without abdicating other aspects of power that he wishes to retain. The key to this strategy is maintaining clear boundaries between the arenas in which he retains his power and those in which he turns it over to his students.

When he says "I will not tell you what to do" and acts consistently on that assurance, he is turning over the power for what happens in that classroom to the students. But by attending every class, listening carefully, setting boundary conditions, and participating minimally but seriously, he is legitimizing the arena in which he has given them power. In other words, he is still the source of authority in the class; it is only by virtue of his authority that the class "matters." He is the "founder" of the class. He provides its constitution (his opening speech). His presence gives "reality" to the class; his participation sustains its seriousness of purpose.

By separating power and authority in his classroom, by retaining his authority and giving up his power, Dr. Ford has created a "democratic classroom": not a classroom that functions democratically, but a classroom founded on the structural principle of democracy (separation of power and authority). This classroom helps students become capable of democratic participation by developing their capacities (and hence character) in a democratic direction.

This environment promotes democratic character development because the student group has to struggle with managing and making productive the power that has been handed to them. They are faced with *determining for themselves* how they will speak and act together; they will thus encounter the distinctive challenges and pleasures of "self-determination." Since the environment in which they are facing these challenges is both stable and safe (unlike, say, the environment during a civil war), they enjoy unusual opportunities for the learning and habit development necessary to participate in a democratic community.

One More Job

But the teacher has one more job to do. To what degree he chooses to focus on this job will depend on his temperament, on how "political" he really is as a teacher, and on how self-conscious he is about the issues I have been discussing in this chapter.

We have seen that students want to be taken care of by their teacher: They will try to get the teacher to take control of the class when things get difficult, and they will treat him as the one and only member of the class whose reactions matter. In sum, they will try to return to him the power he has handed over to them. The teacher's final job is to make the students aware of these behaviors as they manifest themselves. He will try to make them "catch themselves in the act" of trying to return the power he has given them back to him.

When students try to seduce him into taking back control of the class, he can silently resist their ploys, and when they seek his approval he can withhold it easily enough. But he will be more helpful to them if he also sometimes *points out to the students what they are doing.* There is an art to doing this effectively, and it is not easy to convey. Generally, it works best to do it bluntly but without elaboration, making a brief comment but refusing to follow it up with any explanation. (Explanation will be experienced as taking back control of the class—finally "teaching" again.) Let us listen in again on Dr. Ford and his students. They have been discussing King Lear's insistence on having his daughters publicly proclaim their love to him.

Dan: It might seem strange, but I really *can* understand the old king wanting to hear how much his daughters loved him. What I *don't* understand is why he would give up his kingdom in the first place. Especially considering how much he likes power.

Emily: Yeah, I felt the same way. What's going on here? Why does Lear give up his kingdom? It seems irresponsible.

Sarah: That's a good question. What do you think, Dr. Ford?

Dr. Ford: (looks up from his notebook, but says nothing)

Ben: Yeah, Dr. Ford, tell us what you think.

Dr. Ford: (pauses)

The class: (remains silent and waits expectantly)

Dr. Ford: (addressing the group as a whole, and not focusing on Ben or Sarah): I think it's interesting that *that* would be the particular question you want me to answer.

Sarah: What do you mean?

Dr. Ford: (says nothing, resumes writing in his notebook)

Elizabeth: He means we're equating King Lear with him.

This interchange illustrates one of a thousand possible ways a teacher might go about this job. I have selected it because Dr. Ford's response to the students' plea for help is so blunt, pointed, and socially awkward. Without going into more detail, I want simply to stress the significance of this task, and note that it can be done lightly or heavily, occasionally or persistently, cryptically or obviously, or in ways that fall in between these polarities.

But the job needs to be done to some degree to help the students discover their own desire to be governed by a teacher. This is a truly liberating discovery, because only by becoming conscious of this desire can they learn to resist acting on it. Once a group of students learns to inhibit those actions that put the teacher back in charge of the discussion, they can begin to learn to take charge of the discussion themselves. At this point they can start learning to govern themselves as a group of equal yet different human beings.

The Ideal End

The ideal end point of this development, though it is unlikely to be attained in a single course, is for the group to be able to carry on its work *without the presence of the teacher.* For this to happen, the group's own history would have to gradually develop the authority that had previously resided in their teacher. Such a shift would take place slowly and imperceptibly, but at a certain point, their own customs, precedents, and history (the stories of their past) would provide the authority they needed to continue. Along the way, they might change some of their fundamental rules ("amend their constitution") or even rewrite them entirely. Reaching this end point is improbable, but specifying it makes clear the direction of the development we are discussing.

Refusing to "Teach"

Dr. Ford's Shakespeare seminar exemplifies another way of teaching with your mouth shut. This way really does involve the teacher's keeping his mouth closed a great deal under circumstances that invite speaking. But more than that, it involves a difficult and pointed refusal—a refusal to "help" the students in just those ways they most reasonably expect. Refusing to govern is, however, a refusal in the interest of democracy. In the right setting, this refusal can be a powerful educational instrument. But putting students in a challenging environment and leaving them to explore it and struggle with its structure is not easy for a teacher. It requires patience, endurance, and a faith in the students' capacity to develop.

As in each of the chapters of this book, I bring this mode of teaching to your attention, not to propose it as *the* way to teach, but rather to further elaborate what "teaching with your mouth shut" might entail. To round out the picture I have painted, I will outline a continuum of less extreme to more extreme "democratic teaching" practices.

A Continuum of Democratic Teaching Practices

We can place various efforts at promoting democratic participation through teaching along a continuum. On the left, the modest end, lie efforts in which the student's character is pushed in a democratic direction almost as a by-product of learning activities designed for other purposes. On the right, the bold end, are extremely artificial learning environments self-consciously designed with democratic ends in mind. In the middle are most of the teaching activities we would encounter in looking for educational practices that promote self-determination, including Dr. Ford's Shakespeare seminar.

The conceptual workshops discussed in Chapter 6 are a good example of learning activities at the modest end of the continuum. They were designed with conceptual aims in mind, but they do promote the development of mental and behavioral habits that are, generally speaking, democratic. In a conceptual workshop the teacher does tell his students what to do, in great detail, but he tells them in writing, and he leaves them mostly to their own devices to figure out how to carry out his instructions.

A decentralized class where students work in small groups and the teacher wanders around differs dramatically from a class where the teacher commands all the attention from the front of the classroom. The rearrangement of bodies and reorientation of eyes and ears in a conceptual workshop requires students to pay much more attention to each other than to their teacher. They face each other, talk to each other, listen to each other, and usually *the teacher is not even present.* He is off visiting some other group. The teacher has told them what to do, but he cannot enforce his orders because he is not there. So the group must decide to what degree to keep on task, how seriously to pursue the work, and how much to rely on one or two strong "leaders" in the group or how much to share the load equally.

Participating in such groups regularly is bound to affect students' habits and dispositions. Taking part in them promotes thinking and speaking for the sake of understanding, rather than for the sake of the teacher's approval. It fosters habits of group responsibility, mutual aid, and reliance on one's own mind rather than the teacher's.

Students who are regularly placed in conceptual workshop groups will be in a better position to face the challenges of an open-ended seminar than those who are not. This point reinforces what I have repeated so often: No one teaching approach discussed in this book is meant to carry the whole burden of teaching. Most of the modes I have been discussing work best in combination with others, each supporting or complementing the others in specific ways.

At the bold end of the continuum, we find learning environments self-consciously designed to promote democracy and freedom. The late A. S. Neill's school, Summerhill (a school that became well-known through Neill's book *Summerhill,* published in 1960), is one example. At Summerhill, not the classroom but the whole school becomes the locus for democratic practice. No rules are imposed by adults on students. The students govern themselves through "school meetings" where all rules are created through a process of open debate and voting. The school meeting also has to enforce the rules and to decide the consequences of infractions for individual students.

Attendance at classes is not required. What actually happens inside the classroom is not altogether clear, and certainly must be variable, but Neill's book underscores that what was most important to him was not specific subject-matter learning, but rather "learning to be free," and that he tried to implement this aim by making the entire school a radically democratic community.

There is a wonderful documentary on Summerhill, a film dominated by the figure of Neill (as, surely, the school itself was). Neill was a charismatic figure, and clearly he seldom kept his mouth shut. Nevertheless, we have to classify the creation and running of Summerhill as a prime instance of teaching with your mouth shut, for there can be no doubt that what shapes the character of its students more than anything else is their regular participation in meaningful democratic self-governance.

The Self-Reflective Group

Another example of a teaching practice from the bold end of the continuum is an experiment I call the "self-reflective group," a specialized class that I adapted, in my own teaching, from an unusual psychology class I observed at Harvard as a graduate student in the late '60s. The self-reflective group was a much less sweeping and more focused way of trying to promote democracy, one that followed from the analysis of group behavior and transference discussed in this chapter.

Its subject matter was the social psychology of small groups ("group dynamics"). The learning objectives of this class can be stated in several ways; they sound different, but in the context of this class, they mutually require each other: (1) understanding small-group dynamics, (2) learning how to be a participant-observer of a group in which you are a member, (3) learning how to become an effective member of a group that governs itself, (4) grasping the implications of "transference" by learning to detect its results in yourself and in your group, and (5) learning how to "deal with" an authority figure in a group in which the figure of authority refuses to exercise any power.

I hope the reader will see that although these five aims were not the explicit objectives of Dr. Ford's Shakespeare seminar, they are implicit in the way he ran that class. In the self-reflective group, I made the first three objectives explicit and went out of my way to push the students to achieve all five.

The self-reflective group served as an experiential learning "lab" where students learned about group behavior by studying the behavior of their own group. To learn from such a lab requires the development of the difficult skill of becoming a participant-observer of a group in which you are a member. To this end, students were required to (1) spend the last 15 minutes of each two-hour session writing silently in their journals, reflecting on what took place during that particular session; (2) sit silently against the wall as one of five observers for one in every five classes, taking notes on what they observed and discussing their observations with the other observers at the end of the session; and (3) write regular essays on the development of the self-reflective group (these essays were the *only* basis for each student's grade).

My behavior in this group followed the same spirit as Dr. Ford's but was more narrowly focused on the five objectives listed earlier. During the first class, after my opening speech, I refused to speak at all. In subsequent classes, my comments were few, and somewhat in the spirit of Dr. Ford's response to the Lear question. I always addressed my remarks to the group rather than to any individual, and I restricted my comments to interpretations of group behavior, using them particularly to expose the group's unrealistic expectations of me. I never made generalizations and only drew attention to specific behavior that had just happened. In addition, I maintained my own journal and spent most of the class period writing continuously in it, recording all that was going on in the group.

I was also explicit about providing the "constitution" for the group. I started the first class not by waiting, but by handing out a sheet of paper, which I then read aloud to the group, slowly and formally. This paper stated the goals of the group and its basic rules of operation (which mostly revolved around the behavior of observers and their rotation). This document contained the following three key clauses: (1) "I will not tell you what to do"; (2) "Anything that the group does becomes fair game for discussion within the group"; and (3) "Your grade will be *solely* determined by your written essays." (This last restriction was crucial because it meant that what students did or didn't do during class could not affect their grade; technically, they didn't even have to attend—although it would have been impossible to write satisfactory essays if they did not.)

I also ordered the books and provided a syllabus with weekly reading assignments. But I did nothing to enforce these assignments, nor did I do anything to insure that the books were discussed in class. It was up to the students to decide when, how, and how much to discuss the readings, and their decisions on this count varied dramatically from week to week. Over the life of the group, however, discussion of readings occupied only a small proportion of the group's time.

With respect to reading and evaluating the essays, I acted as a normal writing teacher would. My comments urged the students to analyze the group as an organism unto itself, and to resist writing about themselves. (The "self" in "self-reflective group" refers to the group's collective "self" not to the student's individual self, but it took students awhile to figure this out.) My comments also pressed students to supply concrete evidence of the group's behavior to back up any claims they made about the group's development. (Eventually they discovered the value of taking good notes in class.)

When I finished reading the initial handout on the first day of class, I asked if there were any questions and waited. Usually there were not, but if there were any, I answered them. Then I sat down and said, "Okay, then, let's begin." *And then I kept my mouth shut.* For the rest of the two hours. If I was asked a question directly, I simply repeated, "I am not going to tell you what to do," or I deflected the question, saying something like, "There are other people in the room who can answer that question." In subsequent classes, I spoke occasionally, but I kept my comments to a minimum, especially during the early weeks.

By these means, I effected a radical separation of power and authority in the classroom. I turned over all the power to the students to determine what they would do during the hour and forty-five minutes that preceded their journal writing. At the same time, I emphasized my own authority by "founding" the class, providing its constitution, and placing myself at the center of it as a witnessing presence.

By effecting this split so dramatically, I made myself even more an object of special attention than I might otherwise have been. By saying so little, by making terse comments when I spoke, and by writing constantly in my journal, I made myself into a "blank screen," an ideal object for the projection of unconscious feelings and fantasies. The transference reactions that are always at play in a classroom—the yearnings for the teacher to meet all needs, to provide emotional sustenance, to be the ideal parent—became more manifest in speech and behavior than usual. And thus they were harder to ignore. My comments constantly drew attention to these reactions, and eventually students learned to recognize them, first in others, and later in themselves.

There are really three dimensions to the objectives of the self-reflective group. The political dimension aims at developing democratic participation, the anthropological dimension at training students to observe group behavior, and the psychological dimension at helping them identify transference reactions. Since democracy is a particular way of organizing how a group behaves, the political and anthropological objectives obviously converge.

Though the psychological aim might at first seem quite separate, it is not. Transference reactions get in the way of group members' treating each other as equals and thus of establishing a community that is democratic in practice and not just in name precisely because everyone's attention is riveted on the one member of the group whom they refuse to treat as an equal—the teacher. Until they get over him, they cannot really come together as a group, deliberate with each other, hear each other, make decisions, and act together.

Learning how to observe—to hear and see beneath the surface of the group's behavior—enables them to recognize the special treatment afforded the teacher, and this recognition paves the way for a gradual transformation in the behavior of the group. It would take too long to recount here the details of this transformation. In one sentence, the students have to cut the teacher out of the group completely, often literally asking him to leave for a class session, before they can get over him (always a partial process anyway). Only after such a "wrenching" act can they begin to admit him as an "equal" member of the group. (Those interested in this process should consult Philip Slater's *Microcosm.*)

A Shift toward Democracy

By placing four teaching practices on our continuum (open-ended seminar, conceptual workshop, Summerhill, and self-reflective group), I have tried to give a sense of the range of possibilities. Most learning environments, if they belong on the continuum at all, lie in the middle. Collaborative independent research projects, for instance, lean to the left, yet occupy a position closer to the middle than conceptual workshops. Students on a project team must choose their topic and learn how to work together, yet in most cases, the intellectual objective of learning the subject they are researching overshadows the "political" goal of learning how to work together as equals.

In any case, the notion of a continuum is not important other than to indicate that the set of issues I have discussed under the headings "refusing to 'teach'" and "separating power and authority" have a much wider range of application than a discussion of any single teaching instance might suggest. These issues pervade all teaching, but they usually remain unnoticed and undiscussed.

In fact, these issues have been with us since the start of this book. What is "teaching with your mouth shut" if not refusing to do the students' work for them? Telling students what you want them to know rests on a belief in the power of the direct verbal transmission of knowledge. The alternatives I have been discussing in this book originate in a skepticism about this power. As such, they necessitate a refusal on the part of the teacher to do many of the things normally expected of teachers, above all, to do *the* thing expected most of teachers: Telling.

The alternatives examined in this book rest on a faith in *indirection.* We have seen how indirect teaching requires organizing an environment for students and then standing back and letting them interact "freely" in that environment. But the freedom implied is a tempered one since the environment itself has a shape—limits, resistances, opportunities. Once he has designed his environment, the teacher can step back and let the environment "teach" in his stead, knowing it will do so more effectively.

This shift toward indirection is not automatically democratic; one can design different environments for different ends. But the minute we are talking about teaching a group rather than one lone student, the shift that removes the teacher from center stage has an inherently democratic cast to it. Once the teacher steps aside, the students are left with each other. They are left to do their work in the environment the teacher has designed for them, but a crucial aspect of that environment is *their fellow students.*

One way or another they have to learn to deal more directly with their peers; their interactions are no longer all with a teacher (in the presence of peers). They actually have to talk with each other, to write to each other, to inquire together as a community. Compared to the activities of traditional schooling, each of these activities is a step toward building a democratic community, and *learning* how to master these activities involves the students in the development of a democratic character. Thus, teaching with your mouth shut would seem particularly well-suited to societies whose aim is democracy.

A Multitude of Refusals

"Refusing to 'teach'" sounds jarring, and if taken literally, is irresponsible. The quotation marks around the word "teach" attempt to ward off the literal interpretation. But good teaching involves a teacher in a multitude of refusals, often on a daily basis. The experienced teacher will hardly notice them and not think of labeling them as "refusals."

Imagine yourself in the simplest teaching situation: At the end of the term one of your students, Cindy, comes to talk with you in your office. She asks you what career she should pursue after college. Do you simply tell her what vocation to seek?

In some circumstances you might gently suggest a direction, but more than likely you will feel that she is the one to answer that question. You *refuse* to answer it for her; you refuse to "tell her what to do." Rather, you act indirectly. You pose some questions, you start a discussion, you tell a story; in sum, you try to create a situation where she will be able to make the best decision for herself.

Why do you refuse to do her work for her? There are at least two good reasons. First, you think it good for the development of her character to be making the decision herself. Second, you assume that, in the end, Cindy may know better than you what is best for her. Most teachers would respond to Cindy's plea in their office in just this way. This response comes naturally; it seems to flow from an experienced teacher's common sense.

Each of the teaching activities discussed in this book derives from an extension of this same kind of thinking; each is rooted in this same kind of "common sense." Teaching with your mouth shut necessitates refusing to "teach," that is, refusing to exercise some of the power normally expected of those in the institutional role of teacher. It means refusing to meet some of the normal, unspoken expectations of those in the role of student. It requires, instead, finding a hundred different ways of getting students to assume power for themselves, to take responsibility for themselves and their education. But it never means abdicating the authority without which one cannot be a teacher. *Separating power from authority thus lies at the heart of teaching with your mouth shut.* It is the key to the transfer of power from the older generation to the younger. It is the central distinction upon which the *development* of democracy rests.

8

Teaching with a Colleague

What Happens When Two Teachers Enter the Classroom?

In discussing power and authority in the previous chapter, I accepted the traditional assumption that a classroom consists of a group of students and *one* teacher. But what happens to the organization of power and authority when two teachers enter the classroom as equal teaching partners? In Chapter 3, I alluded to this situation by referring to a specific type of team teaching called "collegial teaching," which I called "one of the most dramatic and unusual ways to teach with your mouth shut." In this chapter, I will characterize "collegial teaching," show its consequences for students, and answer the above question. But first let us perform a thought-experiment to see why we would ever think of introducing a second teacher into the classroom.

A Thought-Experiment

Let us go back for a moment to the inquiry-centered course we examined in Chapter 4, *In Search of Socrates,* and perform a simple thought-experiment. The course consisted of twenty-five students and one teacher, all of whom studied the early Socratic dialogues of Plato (and some other books) in order to try to figure out the significance of Socrates' life, death, and puzzling manner of pursuing philosophy.

What made this course "inquiry-centered" was that its teacher did not think he knew the answers to these questions beforehand; I designed the course in order to have a way to tackle these questions *myself.* I also believed that pursuing their own answers to these questions would provide my students a better education than would their absorbing and learning to paraphrase my answers (assuming I had any). I therefore organized the course as a community of inquiry, allowing that each student would come to her own distinctive interpretation of Socrates—which she would have to defend in a written essay at the course's end.

Still, I did not pretend that I was on a level playing field with my students. I admitted to more knowledge of the readings and their historical context, more time spent thinking about them, more familiarity with scholars' analyses of them, and more experience in drawing reasoned conclusions from these kinds of texts. I tried to *use* my knowledge and experience—in the specific ways discussed in Chapter 4—to help my students with their study without trying to dictate the conclusions they would draw from it.

Faced with a course designed in this spirit, a student may still resist its aim. She may conclude that, despite everything, the real game here is to figure out the teacher's answer and give it back to him in the final essay. Such a student, consciously or unconsciously, imposes a cynical interpretation on the course. (Her past experiences in school may give her good reasons for doing so.) She assumes that the teacher really knows the answer to the problem at the center of the course—or thinks he does—but that for educational reasons he wants the students to figure it out for themselves. She assumes the teacher will, consciously or unconsciously, provide clues to this answer along the way, and she therefore focuses all her intelligence on detecting these clues, assembling them together into a coherent whole, and repackaging them as her own "results."

If a student is determined to approach an inquiry-centered course with this attitude, an individual teacher cannot do much to prevent it. Naturally he will have his own ideas about the problem under investigation; inevitably these ideas will be revealed in the course of discussing the course materials. Any student determined to do so will find ample evidence from which to draw conclusions about the teacher's own interpretation. Even though the teacher is trying to teach with his mouth shut, he cannot prevent a student from taking his every word and gesture as a clue to a hidden lecture, nor from taking that hidden lecture as the "knowledge" to be mastered in the course.

But there is a simple and decisive way to undercut this strategy: *Let us introduce a second teacher into the course.* This changes everything. Now there will be two teachers to figure out. Which one should the student focus on? Which one holds the interpretation she should try to root out and master? "Why," she may wonder, "would they put two teachers in one course, anyway?"

Why Would Two Teachers Want to Teach a Course Together?

The student has it wrong: There is no "they" who put two teachers in the same course. In this thought-experiment, the two teachers are sharing one classroom because they want to. They are both interested in Socrates, and they have very different ways of understanding what Socrates was up to. I don't believe Socrates when he repeatedly professes ignorance of the meaning of the philosophical term under investigation in any particular dialogue (e.g., courage, justice, virtue). I find Socrates cagey in making these professions of ignorance—for specific pedagogic and philosophical reasons. But my colleague and fellow teacher (let's call him David) takes Socrates' professions of ignorance seriously. David thinks any reasonable interpretation of Socrates must start from the assumption that he really didn't know the answers to the questions he was pursuing with others in the streets of Athens. He sees Socrates as a *comic* figure with a *political* purpose. I, by contrast, see Socrates as an *ironic* figure with an *educational* purpose.

This much about our differences we had figured out before we began the course. The student's question about "they" must be transformed; the pertinent question is not "Why would 'they' put two teachers in one course?" but "Why do David and Don want to teach this course together?" And the answer is, we want to teach the course together because we share a common interest in the subject matter (Socrates) *and* because we differ in our approach to that subject matter.

This combination—this conjunction of similarity and difference—is what makes teaching together so inviting. *We hope to learn from each other.* Without our common interest, we would have no basis for coming together; but without our intellectual differences, we would be less likely to learn from each other. By inquiring together—reading the Socratic dialogues together, discussing our interpretations, arguing with each other, listening to each other, seeing Socrates through each other's eyes—we expect to learn. By these means we will continue the conversation about Socrates we had begun (in discovering our different orientations) before the course. In a sense, the course will *be* our continued conversation about Socrates.

Where Have All the Students Gone?

But what about the students? The first result of our thought-experiment is that the students seem to have dropped out of sight. But that is not so. They are still part of the course; they just occupy a different position than before. The central activity of the course has now become the intellectual conversation about Socrates carried on by the two colleague/teachers. The students are invited to come along, to listen in and, even better, to join in.

Do not be confused by this language. In the above paragraph I am describing a transformation in the *framework* of the class—in its invisible assumptions. What actually takes place in its day-to-day activities is not very different from what took place when I taught the course alone. The intellectual aim of the course remains unchanged; the reading and essay assignments remain the same. The class activities do not change much. Students continue to participate in conceptual workshops and open-ended seminars.

The one new component is a weekly "faculty panel." This is a class where both teachers present short formal responses (of about 15–20 minutes each) to the same reading. After the two presentations, the teachers continue their "conversation" about the reading informally in front of the students, sooner or later inviting the students to join in the discussion. The teachers also make their panel talks available to the students, later, as written texts to be consulted (see Chapter 5).

This panel serves an essential function beyond contributing new perspectives and interpretations for the students to consider. It makes public the ongoing faculty conversation that is the founding activity of the course. In fact, some students may take the series of weekly faculty panels to *be* that conversation. But really, it is merely the visible and audible portion of a continuous conversation that persists every day of the course. When David and I talk informally, when we make curricular decisions about the course, when we decide what to do tomorrow, when we discuss our students, *even when each of us is thinking about the readings on his own,* we are constantly "talking to each other." We formulate our hypotheses and draw our conclusions in the presence of the other, whether at any given moment that presence be actual, anticipated, or imagined. We each do our own thinking in response to what the other has said yesterday and in anticipation of what the other will say tomorrow. Our conversation about Socrates takes in everything that happens in the course, and lasts, at the very least, from the course's beginning to its end.

The series of weekly panels, then, is both a "sampling" of this conversation (in the statistical sense) and its most formal and public articulation. The students may not be able to formulate in words the pivotal role of the faculty panel in the course, but they feel it. It makes the collegial conversation palpable and serious.

Beyond the addition of this one new weekly activity, the only other differences are that two faculty voices will be heard in the midst of the seminar discussions, two teachers will wander around visiting discussion groups during the conceptual workshops, and all student essays will not be graded by the same teacher. But for the most part, a visitor to this new version of *In Search of Socrates* would see the same activities (plus one) going on during a week as he saw in the old version.

What Difference Does It Make?

If the students have the same objective and do the same work, what difference does it make that David has joined me in the search of Socrates? It makes a huge difference—above all for our imagined cynical student. When teaching alone, I could do nothing to undermine the cynical strategy of a determined student; now, with a colleague at my side, even the most inveterate cynic will find it difficult to hold onto her strategy.

If David and I act as genuine intellectual equals (and we must if the thought-experiment is to succeed), and if we bring genuinely different intellectual perspectives to bear (as we also must for the experiment to succeed), then the cynical student has no way out. Were either of these two crucial conditions not met, she would.

1. If we shared the same views, she could assume that the "correct interpretation of Socrates" was the joint property of both of us, and her job of deciphering it would become easier; she would just have to pool all the clues she collected. So, not only must David and I differ, but we must continually bring out our differences in front of the students.

2. If David and I did not treat each other as respected equals, then she could easily figure out who was the "real" teacher, and who the interloper, and she could ignore the "noise" provided by the latter, keeping her antennae tuned exclusively to the crucial information provided by the former.

But if the two conditions of equality and difference are met, she will have to reassess the situation and change her entire orientation to the course.

Collegial Teaching

While rare, team teaching is not unfamiliar to high schools, and even in colleges one encounters it occasionally. But our thought-experiment has not been about "team teaching." That phrase refers to any arrangement where more than one teacher is responsible for the conduct of one course. One common form of team teaching is based on division of labor. Two teachers divide a course into different parts, and each one teaches half the parts. They need not even be in the same room at the same time to teach the course as a team.

Our thought-experiment was used to spotlight only one specific and unusual kind of team teaching. My colleague Bill Arney and I (in *Educating for Freedom: The Paradox of Pedagogy*—a book we have written on the subject) call it "collegial teaching." Collegial teaching, not team teaching, is the topic of this chapter. It will be helpful (following *Educating for Freedom*) to clarify the nature of collegial teaching by discussing the five criteria that distinguish it from other forms of team teaching. I have already introduced the first two: the presence of equality and of difference between the two teaching colleagues. In fact, all five have been implicit in our thought-experiment. By spelling them out explicitly here, I will demonstrate just what we have accomplished by means of this experiment.

1. The two teachers must be *equal.* They do not have to be equal in status or rank, have equal salaries, or have equal experience teaching. They must simply *respect* each other and treat each other as intellectual equals, whatever differences may exist between them (and there always *will* be differences). Only if the two colleagues genuinely take each other to be intellectual equals will they be able to act as equals before their students.

2. The two teachers must be *different.* They must be *interested* in each other. If there are genuine intellectual differences between them, then there will be a real foundation for each teacher's interest in the way the other construes the subject matter: in the kinds of questions he poses, the kinds of dilemmas he locates, the kinds of resolutions he seeks. Their differences as well as their equality must become visible to their students. But there must *be* differences before any can become visible.

3. The two teachers must act before their students primarily as *intellectual colleagues,* and not as teachers whose main job is to administer a course or deliver a curriculum. Teachers are always, also, administrators. They are administrators of the courses they teach. They have paper to push, rules to enforce, deadlines to meet, order to keep, grades to give—the list is almost endless. A course is like a machine in some respects, and any teacher knows the course won't run smoothly unless he keeps the parts oiled and in motion. No teacher can responsibly avoid this work, and neither can the pair of teachers teaching collegially. But the minute they take these administrative duties to be their *primary* responsibility (as so easily happens), the spirit of collegial

teaching vanishes. A path of least resistance then opens up which can quickly lead to team-teaching by division of labor.

4. A collegially taught course must of necessity be *inquiry-centered* (see Chapter 4). The teachers' primary interest is the collegial conversation—not some predetermined curriculum. This conversation is by its very nature an inquiry into a topic of mutual interest (even if their precise questions about the topic are not the same). The inquiry itself is what draws the colleagues on, not a desire to "cover" a curriculum.

5. Finally, collegial teachers must *conceive of their students in a new way.* They must think of their students as occupying the role of "auditor to the collegial conversation," and, from the beginning, they must invite their students to move into a second role—that of "participant in the collegial conversation." Both these roles require some explanation. Each is readily susceptible to misinterpretation.

Auditors

Because collegial teaching shifts the central activity in a course from "covering a curriculum" to "participating in an inquiry," and because, at the outset, the inquiry has already been launched by the two teachers, the students are displaced from their normal position in the emotional landscape of the classroom. The typical classroom is structured around the student–teacher relationship. Each student has some kind of relationship with her teacher, and each relationship carries a certain emotional weight in making the classroom atmosphere what it is. Thus, each student occupies a position of some importance in the traditional classroom.

But collegial teaching is structured around the teacher–teacher relationship! The students, in a fundamental sense, are displaced. (For a defense of this displacement, consult *Educating for Freedom.*) They become, in a certain sense, outsiders. But they *are* given a role to occupy: They become *auditors,* members of the audience before which the collegial conversation takes place. They can learn a lot from listening carefully to this conversation. In fact, one can argue that a student will learn more by being permitted to listen to a conversation between two teachers than by being *forced against her will* to participate directly, one-on-one, in a conversation with one teacher. Whether or not one buys this argument, it seems indisputable that you can learn a lot about books you have studied by listening with care to an ongoing conversation between two experienced, curious minds about those very books. This is the position that all students are initially placed in when teaching is done collegially.

It was also the position occupied by Plato (and the other young admirers of Socrates) when Socrates carried on his probing conversations with the leading citizens of Athens. And the educational advantage of this position may explain why Plato seemed to learn a lot more from those conversations than did the men directly engaged with Socrates. (It is also the position occupied by children listening to their parents converse at the dinner table.)

But it is easy to draw a false conclusion about this shift in roles for students. It sounds as if students are being shifted from an active role in learning to a passive one. Not so. In the first place, becoming an auditor in a collegially taught course cannot entail becoming a passive recipient of knowledge because the course's inquiry-centered organization abolishes the notion of knowledge-to-be-delivered from the start; knowledge in such a course is rather to be "constructed" (or "discovered" or "invented") by those undertaking the inquiry.

In the second place, when we introduced our second teacher into the course, we abolished none of its learning activities and all of them called for active thinking and engaged participation. Calling the students "auditors" does not restrict them to any particular kind of learning activity; the term characterizes only the overarching relationship between the students and their teachers.

An Invitation to Participate

The full force of collegial teaching derives not from the role of auditor into which students are placed but from a second role they are invited to enter: *participant in the collegial conversation.* By means of this invitation, students are welcomed into, but not forced to enter, the community of inquiry. To enter this community students must meet two requirements.

1. First, they must become *interested* in the inquiry. You can't participate in an inquiry without a "present interest" in it, and you can't fake such an interest. If a student becomes genuinely interested in the question at the center of the course, she will want to pursue it. Then all she has to do is join forces with those already engaged in the inquiry—the two teachers she has been witnessing and any other students who have already joined them.

2. The second requirement is more difficult. *The student must address her teachers not in the voice of "student" but as a colleague.* Within the confines of the collegial conversation, she must renounce the role of "student" and participate as an equal with her teachers. The reason is implicit in the first criterion of collegial teaching. The collegial conversation can only take place among equals, and as anybody knows, a "student" is not equal to a "teacher." These institutional roles have inequality built right into them. Only by stepping out of these roles can

teachers and students come together for a collegial conversation. And this opportunity is exactly what teachers are offering their students in a collegially taught course.

What does it mean for a student to renounce the role of "student" in the midst of a course? It means only that she be willing to talk to her teacher as one person to another—despite the glaring differences in their age, experience, and institutional power. There is no recipe for talking this way, yet there is no mistaking it when a person addresses you in this spirit. Any student who does so is welcomed into the conversation.

Just as it was easy to misinterpret the role of auditor, so too is it easy to misconstrue the idea of "an invitation to participate." For teachers to view their students as potential participants in a collegial conversation might be taken to mean that the teachers will admit them into their conversation only after they have realized some of their potential. One might assume that the teachers have some academic standards that students must meet before they are deemed worthy of joining the conversation. "They must get sufficient background." "They must learn the Basics first." "They must prove they are capable."

Nothing could be further from the spirit of collegial teaching than the holding of such standards for participation in inquiry. The invitation to participate is offered right from the start, and it is genuine. Any student is free to take her teachers up on it at any time. All she has to do is to decide to enter the conversation; the one condition is that she not try to enter it in the role of "student" because the conversation cannot proceed on those grounds. But if she enters it as a colleague, she will be welcomed immediately.

But what about the obvious ways in which she is unequal to her teachers: her lack of knowledge, experience, intellectual facility? These do not matter. When we let a second teacher into *In Search of Socrates,* we required him to pass no tests. I assume that any two teachers joining forces to teach together will be unequal along just those lines listed above. One will know more about the subject; one will be brighter or quicker; one will have more experience teaching, one more in scholarship. A community of inquiry does not require participants of equal skill or knowledge. It only requires people who are willing to treat each other as equals and who bring some interesting differences with them into the community, as will, most likely, each student who seeks to enter the collegial conversation.

And, besides, if the teachers are so smart, why haven't they already solved the problem of Socrates? The very fact that they are working together on a difficult problem that interests them, *and to which they do not know the answer,* creates an equality between them and anyone else interested in the problem and willing to work hard on it. And who is to say that a student with a fresh and unprejudiced approach may not be just the one to solve the problem? The teachers have to be willing to find this a reasonable possibility—as does the student herself. If the three of them can agree that this outcome is plausible (and desirable), then they have already demonstrated their equality.

Accepting the Invitation

The notion that students will renounce the institutional role of "student"—with all its privileges—and join their teachers as colleagues in an intellectual inquiry sounds utopian. Can students really take this step? If offered a genuine invitation in this spirit, how many students will accept it?

The answer to the first question is, yes, some can. As for the second question, some will, some won't, and some will struggle with their own ambivalence, torn between saying "yes" and "no, thank you."

Bill Arney and I have together offered a number of collegially taught courses at our college. The last time we taught such a course (*The Paradox of Freedom*), we explicitly informed our students of our conception of collegial teaching with its pointed invitation for students to join our conversation. We even assigned a draft of our book on collegial teaching as the first reading assignment.

As we expected, our students found this conception of teaching extremely controversial, and they discussed it incessantly. Many students wrote essays about the idea: Some argued that the invitation was a sham, others that it represented an impossibility, still others that it was a difficult but laudable goal. From reading these essays I concluded that the easiest way for students to enter the collegial conversation was through writing, and I "published" an essay in the Class Notebook (see Chapter 5) making that argument.

My experience teaching *The Paradox of Freedom* has informed my answers to the two questions above. Some students took up the invitation with gratitude and gusto right from the start, some took it up slowly and reluctantly, some rejected it out of hand as impossible, some rejected it as undesirable, and many struggled with their own confusion and ambivalence about the whole notion of equality between student and teacher.

But my impression was that, despite this range, the course was educationally beneficial for all but one or two of the students. Regardless of their own personal responses to the invitation to participate, students were forced to reflect on their life as "students" in educational institutions. They were provoked to think more clearly about their reasons for being in college and about the particular posture in which they occupied the role of "student"—a role they have performed for most of their lives.

Such reflection, accompanied as it was by constant discussion both in and out of class, was useful to all categories of students. It prompted their taking a major step forward in attaining the kind of self-knowledge that ought to be a fundamental part of a liberal arts education. And remember that while all this talk was going on about "the possibility of students becoming colleagues with their teachers," the students were still reading books, holding seminars on the books, listening to panel talks, and writing essays regularly. In other words, all the educational opportunities of a "regular" course were present alongside the debate about collegial teaching.

I conclude this section by quoting the words of three students from this course in order to show that, as I said, *some* students are capable of accepting the invitation to participate, and also to show the value of a collegially taught course for one who was not.

These words are taken from the students' evaluations of their teachers. While faculty evaluations are required at The Evergreen State College, there is no form or format for writing them. Students simply face a blank sheet of paper and decide how to address their teacher's work. *The Paradox of Freedom* was a full-time "academic program" (16 credits per quarter) and lasted for two quarters. Students wrote a faculty evaluation at the end of each quarter.

I begin by quoting a student who chose not to accept the invitation to participate. At the course's end, she wrote to me:

> At other schools, and even here at Evergreen, I've felt a certain pressure to be "in" with my faculty, to be one of "those" students that the teachers like and respect above the others. But one of the by-products of my figuring out the nature of this course is that I have become critically unconcerned with our relationship. So I write a few papers, you read them and comment, I see you in seminar and at the panels, and that's it. That's fine. As far as I'm concerned, this course isn't about you and me; it's about me. And I like it that way.

A second student showed herself capable of accepting her teachers' invitation to participate in their conversation easily and right from the start. Here is how she described the experience to my colleague.

> I don't remember much of first impressions, except feeling I had to impress you, or at the very least, convince you to allow me into your class. . . . What I remember about that first meeting is talking. I had to give my spiel: how I wanted to be challenged, read good books and continue writing. Then we talked. Mostly about writing. Mine, and yours. You gave me some of your writing you thought I'd be interested in; I promised some of mine. You handed me the [syllabus] and told me to think about it a while and come back if I was still interested. I came back. Of course. Our talk was a good one.

Finally, here are the words of one student who resisted the invitation to participate for quite some time, but eventually, and to her own surprise, finally accepted it—decisively and irrevocably. These excerpts are taken from two separate evaluation letters to me by the same student, the first written halfway through the course and the second at its completion.

> Fall Quarter: I'm not sure if I ever found what you intended for me to find while reading your book. What I believe you were saying was, "Quit limiting yourself by designating yourself as a student, and join our conversation." I came to the conclusion that, for me, that wasn't fully possible. I wasn't ready to be your colleague and I'm still not ready. Maybe it's because I plan to go to Law school and I don't want to get too far away from being a "good student." I don't want my changed frame of mind as to what a student should be to cause me trouble in Law school.

> Winter Quarter: Finally, I would like to thank you for your invitation to become a colleague. I feel I accepted that invitation during the winter quarter. It felt surprisingly natural and easy to accept and challenging to keep up with it. It was amusing when I found myself defending and explaining your offer to other students. I think some of them still believe it is impossible to become a colleague of yours. I feel honored to know otherwise.

But Is It Teaching with Your Mouth Shut?

When I told Bill Arney that I would be writing a chapter on collegial teaching for this book, he suggested I title it, "Let Your Colleague Do the Talking." Sympathetic readers may agree that collegial teaching represents a novel approach to running a high school or college course; they may even grant its educational value. But surely they will wonder: Is it really an instance of teaching with your mouth shut?

I think it is. You may recall that I called it "one of the most dramatic and unusual ways to teach with your mouth shut." But at first glance, it does not sound like it. The central and founding activity of the course is a *conversation* between teacher/colleagues held in front of their students. These teachers are talking. They are talking to each other (and to students), and students (the "auditors") are listening to them talk.

What is more, the teachers' talk is not some indirect form of speech that, as in previous chapters, can avoid the label of "Telling." It is direct talk about the course's subject matter: reasoned arguments in speech and writing about the problem at the center of the course. In a sense collegial teaching is teaching-through-Telling twice over. It presents students with the Telling of not just of one teacher, but of two.

But it is just this doubling that justifies my "yes" answer to the question. Teaching-through-Telling cannot really proceed through two separate voices if they present different points of view. For collegial teaching to work, the two colleagues must *differ*. If they differ, then a student cannot "learn" simply by mastering what she has been told, because her teachers have told her two opposing things. At the very least, she must choose between them; at the best, she will start to think for herself and develop a third point of view. At the very best, she will join her teachers in their conversation in order to convey that third point of view.

Even if a student decides that one and only one of her two teachers is in possession of the truth, the presence of two teachers makes a difference. The student has still had to *decide on her own* which of the two teachers to heed. She has to exercise some independent judgment in making this one decision. And she has to reject the authority of one of her teachers in order to accept the authority of the other.

Paradoxically, the two voices-that-Tell cancel each other out. And that is why teaching with a colleague (in the manner here described) *is* a form of teaching with your mouth shut. It "lets the inquiry do the talking."

The Only Freedom of Enduring Importance

When two colleagues join together to teach a course collegially, they are not only creating the conditions for a stimulating intellectual adventure and the possibility of a long-term friendship; they are also *automatically* effecting that separation of power and authority in the classroom that we found in Chapter 7 to be necessary for an education in democracy. By coming together in front of students, each of the two teachers turns over to students, whether he intends to or not, that form of power most important to freedom: the power to make up your own mind.

By starting a public dialogue with his colleague, he puts before his students a set of choices: What will they choose to believe? How will they assess the knowledge offered to them as the truth? On whom will they rely when forced to make judgments? Confronting such questions is fundamental to a democratic education. Collegial teaching automatically faces students with decisions like these. The mere presence of more than one teacher does the trick. (No one has thought to question the suitability for democracy of an education system predicated on the "tyranny" of the single teacher in control of his classroom.) Collegial teaching by its very nature bequeaths from teacher to student that power to think for yourself that John Dewey called "the only freedom that is of enduring importance."

But it does so at no expense to the teachers' authority. Under collegial teaching the authority of the teacher is neither abandoned nor weakened. Rather, it is localized and made plural. Instead of facing the monolithic Authority of the lone teacher—an authority so easily confused with power—students are faced with two "local" authorities. Each teacher speaks with the authority of his own knowledge and experience. The authority of each is felt by students as they witness their other teacher respecting and responding to the authority of his colleague. But the doubling of authority is also decentralizing and helps students distinguish it from power.

The structure of collegial teaching reveals how different authority is from power. In introducing a second teacher into our course, we weakened decisively the power that any teacher could wield over the minds of his students. But we did not sabotage the structure of authority in the course. Our thought-experiment shows us how distinct power and authority really are. It shows us another way that power and authority can be separated in a classroom.

9

Conclusion
Providing Experience, Provoking Reflection

Give Your Pupil No Verbal Lessons

> Dare I expose the greatest, the most important, the most useful rule of all education? It is not to gain time but to lose it.

> All the instruments [of education] have been tried save one, the only one precisely that can succeed: well-regulated freedom.

> Do not give your pupil any kind of verbal lessons; he ought to receive them only from experience.

In these words and more, Jean-Jacques Rousseau created one of the two greatest thought-experiments in education known to Western letters (the other being Plato's *Republic*). In his *Emile, or On Education* (written in 1762), Rousseau constructs a perfect education for a contemporary middle-class European boy. This education is premised on Rousseau's certainty that Nature makes people good, and that Society corrupts them. As Rousseau puts it in the book's first sentence, "Everything is good as it leaves the hands of the Author of things; everything degenerates in the hands of man."

Rousseau names the imaginary boy he will educate "Emile" and he casts himself as Emile's tutor. He considers the job of educating Emile so important and daunting that he makes it the tutor's sole occupation for Emile's entire childhood and adolescence, and he gives the tutor no other pupil but Emile. In addition, he requires that Emile be taken from his parents, away from the corruptions of city life, to be raised in the relative seclusion of the countryside, where he and his tutor ("Jean-Jacques") will live together alone (along with the necessary servants). Since this is only a thought-experiment (or a work of fiction), Rousseau can take extreme measures; as a writer he need make no compromises.

The radical education that Jean-Jacques provides for Emile rests on four pillars: (1) the child's *natural* development, (2) an extended (though ultimately temporary) removal of the child from society and its evil influences, (3) a supportive personal relationship between tutor and student, and (4) the tutor's careful supervision of the child's environment. Since Rousseau believes that Nature makes no errors with children ("the first movements of nature are always right"), we might think he would be satisfied with removing his charge from society and setting him free in the woods and fields to grow up on his own. The first three pillars, or perhaps even the first two, would seem to suffice. Why does Jean-Jacques need to strictly supervise Emile's environment?

Lending Nature a Helping Hand

Rousseau does not provide the answer to this question explicitly, but the details of his book make it obvious. Emile is to learn not from verbal instruction or admonishment but from *experience.* But rich as it is, experience is not automatically instructive. Running around wildly and blindly in the woods will not yield an education. Emile can learn almost all he will need to lead a good and happy life from experience, but he will require some assistance. That is why he has a tutor.

Although the tutor's primary job is *negative*—protecting Emile from destructive experiences (mainly social and verbal)—Jean-Jacques also has a *positive* function. He needs to make sure that (a) certain kinds of experiences actually happen to Emile, and (b) when they do, Emile will learn from them. As powerful, good, and instructive as Nature is, she cannot educate Emile all by herself; a teacher is also needed to lend Nature a helping hand.

Here are two strikingly different examples. To provoke Emile to learn some rudimentary astronomy, Jean-Jacques takes him out into a field to observe the rising sun. The following passage (written as advice to the tutor) illustrates both the manner and spirit in which Jean-Jacques lends Nature a helping hand.

> On this occasion, after having contemplated the rising sun with him, after having made him notice the mountains and the other neighboring objects in that direction, after having let him chat about it at his ease, keep quiet for a few moments like a man who dreams, and then say to him, "I was thinking that yesterday evening the sun set here and that this morning it rose there. How is that possible?" Add nothing more. If he asks you questions,

do not respond to them. Talk about something else. Leave him to himself, and be sure that he will think about it.

Emile might have noticed on his own the discrepancy between where the sun rises and where it sets, and he might then have asked himself the question Jean-Jacques laconically poses to him. But he might also *not* have noticed this discrepancy, or having noticed it, he might not have puzzled over it. In the former case, he would have missed out on an experience crucial to learning; in the latter, he would have had the experience, but he would have learned nothing from it. His tutor makes sure that he gets both the experience and the opportunity to learn from it. These are his two crucial positive contributions to the education Nature provides Emile.

The second example shows the tutor playing the same role in Emile's learning of social concepts. One day Jean-Jacques encourages Emile to plant some beans on a bare patch of land they come across. Day after day they tend the beans with loving care, eagerly anticipating the green shoots. One day, to his horror, Emile finds his bean plot upturned and destroyed. Who could have perpetrated this vicious deed? When the dust settles, it turns out that the responsibility lies with the gardener, Robert, whose land Emile had unknowingly used. Robert is furious with Jean-Jacques and Emile: They have trespassed on *his* land and destroyed *his* garden—a garden in which he had planted some "exquisite melons." What were they thinking?

The result is anguish: "Tears flow in streams. The grieving child fills the air with moans and cries." But when the tears are over, Jean-Jacques and Emile have plenty of time (at this point in his education, they are "losing time, not gaining it") to talk over what happened. Emile will have many questions. Jean-Jacques will help him discover the answers. Together they will reflect on the experience they had. And from that reflection Emile will construct for himself a preliminary understanding of the complex social concept "private property."

Of course, Jean-Jacques and Robert had hatched this plot from the start. Considerable artifice and planning may be required sometimes to make sure that Emile has the right experience. But even in this more complicated case, the teacher is contributing to the student's education in the same two ways. He is *providing an experience,* and he is *provoking reflection* on that experience.

Over and over, Rousseau's book illustrates the need for a teacher to carry out these two functions. But he never discusses education explicitly in these terms. The philosopher who does is John Dewey, who went further than anyone in spelling out a philosophy of education grounded in experience.

No Idea Can Be Conveyed from One Person to Another

In *Democracy and Education* (published in 1916), Dewey applied a distinctively American progressive philosophy to education. He starts from the assumption that our normal condition is one of ongoing interaction (guided by habit) with our environment. Our habits reflect what intelligence we have, and thus how successful our interactions are in meeting our needs (see Chapter 4).

But Dewey distinguishes between *intelligence* and *thinking*. We always manifest our intelligence, else, failing to meet our basic needs, we would not survive. But we *think* only when some obstacle arises, preventing the satisfaction of our needs and throwing us into disequilibrium. In other words, intelligence organizes our experience, while thinking is our means for reflecting on that experience—in order to modify our intelligence through a change of habits.

From these premises, Dewey draws a shocking conclusion.

> . . . no thought, no idea, can possibly be conveyed as an idea from one person to another. When it is told, it is, to the one to whom it is told, another given fact, not an idea. The communication may stimulate the other person to realize the question for himself and to think out a like idea, or it may smother his intellectual interest and suppress his dawning effort at thought. But what he *directly* gets cannot be an idea. Only by wrestling with the conditions of the problem at first hand, seeking and finding his own way out, does he think.

When someone tells you an idea, he is merely contributing to the stuff of your experience (what Dewey calls a "fact"). If you already have the idea, you can assimilate it without thinking and proceed. If you do not have the idea, you can (a) ignore it, (b) misunderstand it in such a way that it resembles an idea you do have, or (c) stop to think about it. This third possibility is the only case in which the flow of experience is interrupted and reflection commences. But for communication to succeed in this instance, you must develop the idea for yourself (by reorganizing your previous thinking). If you succeed, it may appear that the other person *gave* you the idea. But this appearance is deceptive. The other person only set up the conditions for you to construct the idea for yourself. If this is "giving," it is *indirect* giving. No person, according to Dewey, can *directly* convey an idea to another person.

Dewey's whole philosophy of education flows from this radical conclusion. People learn only by thinking for themselves; the teacher's task is to set up conditions that provoke thinking (as Jean-Jacques did for Emile).

To do so, the teacher must understand how thinking is organized and how it connects to experience. After discussing these matters at length, Dewey summarizes his results in these words.

> . . . the important thing is that thinking is the method of an educative experience. The essentials of method are therefore identical with the essentials of reflection. They are first that the pupil have a genuine situation of experience — that there be a continuous activity in which he is interested for its own sake; secondly, that a genuine problem develop within this situation as a stimulus to thought; third, that he possess the information and make the observations needed to deal with it; fourth, that suggested solutions occur to him which he shall be responsible for developing in an orderly way; fifth, that he have the opportunity and occasion to test his ideas by application, to make their meaning clear and to develop for himself their validity.

Dewey's language is dry, but his insights are penetrating. A careful reading of this paragraph will give a teacher all the "facts" she needs — if she can reflect on them and turn them into her own ideas — to figure out how to teach with her mouth shut. They have guided my own thinking from the beginning.

In earlier chapters I argued that the secret to teaching without Telling lies in setting students free in an environment that has been carefully designed to be instructive. This is a more general way of characterizing what Dewey advises in the excerpt just quoted. My present formulation, "providing experience, provoking reflection," supplements my earlier one by suggesting that the environment a teacher designs should prompt two different kinds of outcomes, each in its proper time.

First, it should yield a potentially instructive experience, one that provokes thinking because it causes some disequilibrium. Second, it should allow for thinking about that experience, reflection that aims to fathom its meaning. If successful, the reflective effort will result in an increase in intelligence (however small): It will yield more fruitful habits of response. These new habits, in turn, enable the pupil to have new and more meaningful experiences from the same environment. In this way, a teacher can help intelligence to develop.

Once these ideas are understood, they can be summarized by the phrase I have used in this chapter's title: "providing experience, provoking reflection." A teacher can teach by providing her students with instructive experiences and by provoking them to reflect on the meaning of those experiences.

In a nutshell, this is the secret to leaving Telling behind. Dewey's point of view, when put into practice, leads directly to teaching with your mouth shut. It has informed every chapter of this book.

Great Books Engender Experience

The power of a great book (see Chapter 2, "Let the Books Do the Talking") is precisely that it can provide a powerful educational experience for a group of students. The teacher is providing an instructive experience for students simply by getting them to read the book.

Reading *is* an experience; books stimulate imaginative experience in their readers. Great books stimulate rich experiences we can learn from. But we don't automatically learn just by reading. How many books have we read and enjoyed that we can't even remember! And even many we remember fondly did not provoke us to significant learning.

A great book tends, all by itself, to provoke reflection on its contents. Through different means at different times, the *Iliad* invites its readers to pause, establish some distance, and think about their experience of the poem. In Chapter 2 we examined two different reflective questions the poem puts before its audience.

However, it is not enough to be questioned. We must take the time to ponder the questions and try to address them. And we will usually need some help. So a teacher must not only provide an experience by getting us to read the book, she must also provide an occasion (and a framework) for reflecting on that experience. There are many ways to do that in a school setting. The most typical are class discussion, essay assignments, exams, and even lectures (but see below for the reason lectures usually fail at this job).

The distinction between experience and reflection is not absolute. Reflecting, after all, is an experience, too. It would be more precise to distinguish between "immediate experience" and "reflective experience." To immediately experience a concrete scene, a problem, a text, a work of art, means to focus on it alone, to be open to its possibilities, to be dominated by its particular logic and force, to be driven by its peculiar tensions, questions, ambiguities. By contrast, to reflectively experience it is to make connections within the details of the work of the problem, to see it through the lens of abstraction or theory, to generate one's own questions about it, to take more active and conscious control in understanding it.

While not absolute, the distinction is both meaningful and important, pointing as it does to two opposite ends of a spectrum that characterizes our manner of engaging the world around us. Great books provide an immediate experience. They also attempt to engender reflective experience. However, a teacher's assistance can sustain reflection and make it fruitful.

Class Discussion as Reflection

The open-ended seminar discussed in Chapter 3 ("Let the Students Do the Talking") allows students to learn directly from each other, while still under the guidance of a teacher. In Dewey's terms, the entire process of the open-ended seminar is a sustained means of provoking reflection on the experience of reading a book. All the particulars I outlined in Chapter 3, from the opening ritual to the many forms of teacher intervention, serve this single purpose. In getting her students to read the book, the teacher provides an experience for them; in offering them the opportunity for extended discussion of the book's meaning via the open-ended seminar, she provokes them to reflect on that experience.

Inquiry: A Rhythm of Experience and Reflection

Chapter 4 ("Let Us Inquire Together") examined the kind of course that best supports the activities discussed in Chapters 2 and 3. Organized as a group inquiry into a question of common interest, the inquiry-centered course fits Dewey's vision perfectly. The teacher is responsible for providing both experiences and opportunities for reflection. She must orchestrate a satisfying rhythm of activity in which immediate intellectual experience alternates with reflection on that experience. The details will depend on the subject matter, the teacher, and the students.

The many activities of *In Search of Socrates* constituted such a rhythm. Students completing this course felt they had had a firsthand encounter with Socrates; they also spent hundreds of hours reflecting on the many possible meanings of that encounter. And because Plato's dialogues bring Socrates to life so powerfully, their encounter with Socrates felt personal to the students, making their need to reflect all the more pressing. It motivated them to stick with their search for Socrates through innumerable frustrations. They were, in the end, trying to make sense of something puzzling and profound that *each of them had experienced.*

Writing as Reflection *and* Experience

One of the most effective means for reflecting on experience is writing. Part I of Chapter 5 ("Speaking with Your Mouth Shut: The Art of Writing") explored different kinds of teacher-generated writing. Formal essays written for students, or lectures subsequently made available as written texts, are direct and straightforward ways to assist reflection. Their advantages over the traditional lecture derive from how they more successfully aid reflection. Since written documents can be read at the student's own pace, re-read and studied, and discussed by several students all of whom share a common copy, they allow reflection to go further and to proceed with a greater chance of success.

Writing letters to students in response to their essays is a more complex instance of provoking reflection. The teacher writes to get the student to reflect, but to reflect on what? Is the student supposed to reflect on an *experience?* Surely the teacher is trying to get the student to reflect on his *essay.* She wants him to develop a critical eye to apply to his own writing. She wants him to be able to detect its strengths and weaknesses in order to figure out *what to do* in order to write more effectively.

"What to do" . . . This phrase signals an often overlooked connection: Beneath any product lies a process that made it. It does no good to reflect on a product you have made—a written essay—unless you can carry that reflection all the way back to the experience of making that product, of writing the essay. After all, the purpose of reflecting in this case is to figure out how to write better the next time. The teacher wants her letter to help the student think about *what he did, how he did it, and what he failed to do while he was actually writing his essay.* In other words, the letter is intended to provoke reflection on the experience of writing. Reflecting on the essay itself is just a way station on the path back to thinking about the activity of writing.

But doesn't the teacher's personal letter of response also provide a direct experience for her student, that of reading the letter? Yes, it does. The line between experience and reflection is not hard and clear. The response letter fulfills both functions: It provokes reflection *and* it provides an experience. But the reflection and the experience are about two different things. The reflection is about the student's writing. The direct experience is part of the student's *ongoing personal relationship with his teacher.* If he took the time to reflect on his experience reading the letter (rather than just using the letter as an instrument to reflect on something else), he would find himself thinking about his teacher and his relationship to his teacher, and if he kept going, he would probably end up musing on his career as a student and his many past experiences with different teachers.

The writing community described in Part II of Chapter 5 provides a sustained way of helping students develop one of the strongest instruments of reflection they have at their disposal: writing. In addition, the activities that constitute the writing community provide students with many experiences that are both immediate and reflective, often both at the same time (but, again, about different things). Reading a fellow student's essay will help a student reflect on the course's subject matter. It also provides a direct reading experience that the student must reflect upon in order to write back to the essay's author. And the same may be said of the author's experience reading that response letter. The writing community thus interweaves experience and reflection as it serves to sharpen writing ability—a key tool for reflection of almost any kind.

Designed Experiences

The conceptual workshops described in Chapter 6 ("Experiences That Teach: Creating Blueprints for Learning") are self-consciously designed both to provide experience and provoke reflection. They begin with concrete scenarios or cases so that the students can start with an imaginative experience: in some cases a vivid picture or scene, as in "the Canary Problem," in others, specific passages from books they have just read, as in "*Aporia*." The worksheet then moves the students from direct experience to reflection, often taking them through several cycles of this alternation.

These cycles are built into the written sequence of questions. However, because the students attack these questions as a group, their intellectual experience is also a social one. Each student has to take into account not only what he imagines and thinks, but the thoughts and experiences of his classmates. In reflecting on the fact that a classmate thinks differently about the flight of a bird in a sealed bottle (a social fact), a student will be stimulated to reexamine his own conception of that flight (a personal, cognitive fact). In the conceptual workshop, the two sides of experience come together to promote learning.

Political Experience

The "political classroom" described in numerous variants in Chapter 7 ("Refusing to 'Teach': Separating Power and Authority in the Classroom") is designed expressly to provide a certain kind of experience for its students. The experience of sitting before a teacher who refuses to "teach," but who expects the class to proceed without his leadership is both novel and unbalancing. Its *raison d'être* is precisely to give the students an experience to reflect upon.

This is experiential learning at its most striking. The students find themselves enmeshed in an extended experience that is puzzling and, at times, disturbing. By reflecting on this experience, something the teacher helps them do in many ways, they can learn a great deal about themselves, about the institution of schooling, about the difference between power and authority, and above all, about how to become an effective member of a self-governing group of equals. The extreme version of the political classroom called "the self-reflective group" dramatically illustrates the kind of teaching Dewey is urging. If you go back to Dewey's summary on page 152 and apply it directly to the self-reflective group as described in Chapter 7, you will discover a perfect fit.

Witnessing and Joining In

Collegial teaching, as it is described in Chapter 8 ("Teaching with a Colleague"), creates a learning situation that appears distant from Dewey's ideal. The displacement of students from a central position in the landscape of the classroom by the two teacher/colleagues would seem to water down the students' experience. We might feel that they are witnessing someone else's intellectual experience rather than having their own.

But let us think again. Surely this emotional displacement is itself an experience to reflect on. In addition, the students are having a new experience by witnessing something they may never have seen before: the collegial conversation taking place in front of them and for them. Finally, their urgent and frequent discussions about "the invitation to join the conversation" demonstrate that they find themselves plunged into a new and puzzling experience, one making reflective discussion imperative. In a collegially taught course, students find plenty of experiences to reflect on.

Moreover, any student who takes up the faculty invitation to renounce the role of student and join the conversation at the center of the course undergoes a profoundly new experience. What could be more singular than a student's addressing his teacher as an equal day after day? This, too, will provide much to reflect on, and from this reflection can come learning of lasting significance. This experience, suitably reflected on, could alter forever a student's orientation to authority, as well as to those in power. It could result in the visible development of his character toward a democratic ideal.

An Unheeded Principle

> That education is not an affair of "telling" and being told, but an active and constructive process, is a principle almost as generally violated in practice as conceded in theory. Is not this deplorable situation due to the fact that the doctrine is itself merely told? It is preached; it is lectured; it is written about.

So wrote Dewey in 1916. It is shocking to read that more than eighty years ago the principle that education is a constructive process, not one based on telling and being told, was generally "conceded" but not generally practiced. Today this principle is neither generally conceded nor generally practiced. Why have Dewey's insights gone unheeded?

In fact, Dewey's work achieved great popularity in the United States during the period between the two World Wars. He was widely read and widely regarded as an eminent and wise educational thinker. The popularity of his work spawned the "progressive education movement" of that period. Yet today, teachers in training rarely read Dewey, and the word "progressive" when applied to education has become just a vague abstraction.

The social critic Paul Goodman had an astute explanation for the vanishing of Dewey's legacy: The progressive revolution in education was one of a host of revolutions that were "half-tried" and then deemed to have failed. Dewey's ideas were misunderstood and watered down by the majority of the well-meaning teachers who launched progressive schools during this era. The excesses and sloppy procedures of "free schools" and "progressive education schools" eventually left a permanent blot on Dewey's reputation and a general consensus that progressive education had been tried and found wanting.

If one detects Dewey's influence in schools today at all, it is in elementary school classrooms, and the recent influence on teachers of Jean Piaget is responsible. Piaget spent a lifetime studying how children's conceptual understanding develops, and from this study formulated a psychology of intelligence that fits perfectly with Dewey's philosophy of education. Whether he knew it or not, Piaget's psychological theory of intellectual development rests firmly on the philosophical foundation established by Dewey. In the '60s and '70s, Piaget's work had a major influence on elementary schoolteachers, but, as fads in education inevitably change, that influence too has waned in the face of alleged "advances" in psychological research.

Dewey's vision of education never had a widespread impact on high school or college teaching. Those are the areas where "telling and being told" have always been most entrenched, most taken for granted. Teachers have always found it hard to grasp how an experiential approach could be used without bringing physical materials into the classroom. Abstract subject matter thus seemed resistant to a "hands-on" approach to learning.

In this book I have addressed this problem head on. I have described many different ways that higher learning can be grounded in "intellectual experience," experience that is concrete, vivid, and engaging, involving as it does the "handling" of words, images, and imagined physical situations rather than wooden blocks, flowing water, and rolling marbles. There are many ways to have a perplexing experience in the high school or college classroom, and students can always learn from such and experience through reflection.

Why Telling Fails

In the first chapter, I said I was not aiming to discredit the great charismatic lecturer. Rather, I said, I just wanted her to make room in the spotlight for other varieties of great teachers. I have tried to advocate teaching with your mouth shut without condemning those who teach through the eloquent and persuasive use of speech.

But Dewey's explanation above ("the doctrine itself is merely told. It is preached; it is lectured; it is written about") implies that Telling is ineffective in producing significant change in human behavior. We are now in a position to understand why. Dewey's fundamental argument is not that we *can* learn by reflecting on experience, but rather that this is the *only* way we learn. There are thus two simple reasons why lecturing usually fails to produce significant learning.

First, *lecturers typically presume experience in their students that the students have not actually had.* Most lectures are attempts to organize, draw conclusions from, make connections within, and in general reflect upon some body of experience. These lectures do not *provide* that experience; they assume that the experience is already in the possession of their listeners, either because they have read about it, been told about it, or somehow acquired it in their life.

Occasionally, this assumption may be well-founded for a small number of students, but rarely for the majority. Even if they have read the assignment on which the lecture is based, rarely have they read it with the care necessary to transform the reading into a puzzling experience demanding reflection. The typical college or high school reading assignment does not begin to have effects like those that Plato's dialogues produced in the *In Search of Socrates* students (see Chapter 4). A reading assignment is usually just something to get through, and if it touches the student at all, it touches him superficially. When reading engenders a profound experience, then a lecture *can* be effective, precisely to the degree that it helps the student reflect on that experience.

This last sentence signals the second reason why Telling is usually ineffective. In the typical lecture, *the reflecting is done by the lecturer, not by the student.* I just said that a lecture can be effective "precisely to the degree that it helps the student reflect." I did not say "to the degree that it does the reflecting for him." Dewey's shocking conclusion that "no idea can possibly be conveyed as an idea from one person to another" means that reflecting can only be done for yourself; no one else can do it for you. Yet, usually doing it for the students is just what a lecturer is trying to do.

Under the right conditions, however, the lecturer's ideas can be useful "facts" for the students in the audience; then they can use these facts as grist for their own reflection, and arrive at satisfying conclusions—perhaps the very ones the lecturer had arrived at herself.

Lecturing, then, will work if (a) the students have actually had the experiences germane to the lecture, and (b) the lecturer's words help the students reflect for themselves on those experiences. When these conditions are met, lecturing can be an admirable teaching tool. Unfortunately, they are rarely met.

"The Medium Is the Message"

Paul Goodman has given one explanation of why Dewey's ideas have not taken hold. In Chapter 1, I gave another. I said that to most teachers Telling just comes naturally; in computer terminology, Telling is their "default setting." In the absence of any other consciously chosen approach, teachers fall back on what comes naturally: explaining. In the passage above, Dewey gives a third reason. Even during a time when his principles were "generally conceded," they were violated in practice, because, Dewey says, the progressive doctrine was "itself merely told" to teachers.

When people are in challenging situations, they tend to get anxious. And when people get anxious they tend to fall back on ways of acting that they know from their earliest models. Teaching is a challenging situation, and that is why most teachers teach in the ways they were taught. If you have been subjected to Telling most of your life as a student, you will probably end up teaching through Telling—*even if what you have been told is that Telling is ineffective.* The medium is a stronger message than the message itself.

Teachers are not doomed to teach as they have been taught, but they must make a forcible and sustained effort to break out of the old mold. Most teachers have so much to do just to meet their daily responsibilities that they lack the energy for a break with the past. Since the principle that "education is not an affair of 'telling'" is itself merely told, Telling continues to dominate our classrooms.

But if Telling is ineffective, why then did Dewey devote so much of his life to writing books, and why have I written this book? I cannot answer the first question, since I cannot speak for Dewey, but I will address the second.

I have not written this book expecting that a single reading of it will lead many people to change the way they teach. I have written this book to raise questions, to widen horizons, and to stimulate reflection on our culture's cherished conceptions of "great teachers" and "great teaching." I hope to provide new ground on which concerned parents, citizens, public leaders, teachers, administrators, and students themselves can stand in order to imaginatively criticize what is going on in our high schools and colleges—and what is *not* going on in them. I have not written this book to prescribe how teachers ought to teach. Even though they have been drawn from real teaching practice, my examples, scenarios, case studies, and stories are best taken as thought-experiments.

Following My Own Advice

However, it is possible for this book to be more than an occasion for "telling and being told." It *could* lead to a significant reorganization in the way any particular reader thinks about teaching and learning, and it could even lead a teacher to transform the way she teaches. But in order for the book to have lasting effects on a reader, the conditions for learning summarized in this chapter must be fulfilled. For some readers, reading this book could be an engaging experience that stimulates perplexity or disequilibrium, and they could go on to *learn* from that reading experience by taking the time to carefully reflect on it.

I have tried to satisfy the first condition by interweaving my argument with concrete teaching scenes and specific learning situations. I have hoped that these would stimulate imaginative experiences in my readers, drawing them in and unsettling them to some degree. But even so, I have met only the first of the above two conditions, and this condition is insufficient to bring about significant learning. You will only learn from a reading experience if you take the considerable time needed to reflect on it and construct its meaning for yourself. That is a step you must take on your own. I cannot do it for you. All I can do is make a suggestion or two and provide a tool for reflection.

The best way to reflect on a book is to find at least one other reader of it who also wants to reflect on it. If you can find two or three, so much the better. Then, you need to meet and discuss the book in the serious but informal manner of the open-ended seminar described in Chapter 3. You don't need a leader or a teacher; you can do it on your own.

To improve the chance of successful reflection, two other things will help. First, a re-reading of the book will multiply the fruits of the discussion manyfold. Second, some simple organizational device will help you use your discussion time more efficiently. Any plan will do; the point is simply to avoid becoming scattered by trying to talk about too many different ideas or examples at the same time.

Those are my suggestions for reflection. But I have also taken a further step and provided a conceptual workshop for those who want go deeper. In Chapter 6 I described how conceptual workshops help students to reflect on and learn from books they have read in common. To stay consistent with the spirit of my own book, I have designed one for you. The workshop is designed for either an individual reader or a small discussion group of two or more. You will find the worksheet in the Appendix following this chapter.

The above two avenues for reflecting on this book are complementary: The conceptual workshop will prod you to think about what *I* find most important in this book; the open-ended discussion will allow you and your friends to discover what *you* find most important in it. You may discover implications I have overlooked; you may find that the framework you bring to the book leads you to discoveries I never anticipated.

Creating "Circumstances"

Teaching with your mouth shut entails (a) avoiding the natural temptation to teach through Telling, and (b) providing students with instructive experiences and then provoking them to reflect on those experiences. Beneath the simplicity of these phrases lie a surprising variety and complexity of "circumstances" that can lead to learning. In these pages I have detailed a number of them that are suitable to the high school or college classroom.

The only limits to how far a teacher may go in "creating circumstances that lead to significant learning in others" are (1) her own imagination, and (2) the practical constraints within which she must operate. It is this second limit that teachers will immediately cite in defense of their traditional methods. However, I have found that most teachers exaggerate the degree and severity of their constraints. Teachers who *temporarily* put aside their sense of being restricted in order to *imagine* how they would teach under ideal conditions usually find inventive ways to approximate their ideal teaching situation. What they devise may fall short of perfection, but it is usually satisfying to them and useful to their students.

The Last Word

If one day you should meet me at a social function and ask me what I do, you will now be in a better position to understand the kinds of activities I am referring to when I say, "I teach college."

But I want to end this book on you, not me. Recall the "significant learning moments or events" you described in Chapter 1 in response to my "simple test." (If you did not take the time to remember some, you have another opportunity to do so now.) Find your written notes, or if you can't get your hands on them, think back to what you described. Do the events or moments fit the twofold description that constitutes the title of this chapter: Did you have a perplexing experience, and did you sometime later reflect back on it in order to make sense out of it? If your learning experiences were to be included in this book, in which of the chapters, if any, would they find their logical home?

I have no way of knowing your answers to these questions. I am optimistic in hoping that your answer to the first question will be "yes." If so, you can derive a sense of closure by returning to where you started and finding a deeper meaning in some things in your life you were already familiar with. But even if your answer is "no," reflecting back on those experiences should be useful. It will give you one small way to test the point of view of this book against your own experience, and either revise or develop this book's point of view to make room for your experience, or answer me by providing an alternative point of view that does make sense of your experience. As is always the case, the reader, not the author, gets the last word.

Appendix
Follow-Up to Chapter 9

The following conceptual workshop is designed for individuals or small discussion groups of two or more readers of this book. It will probably take an individual about three hours to answer all the questions in a thoughtful manner; a group will likely take four hours. A shorter version may be profitably done by skipping Part III. The worksheet may also be broken up so that each part is undertaken at a separate session. Special instructions for group work are contained in square brackets.

A CONCEPTUAL WORKSHOP ON *TEACHING WITH YOUR MOUTH SHUT*

Part I: "Circumstances"

1. In Chapter 1 you were asked to describe in writing "two or three of the most significant learning experiences [in or out of school] you ever had." These were characterized as "moments (or events) in which you discovered something of lasting significance to your life."

   If you answered this question at that time, locate your notes or call to your mind the moments you described. Select one of these you would like to think about further. Now, write a fleshed-out version of that moment or event, supplying sufficient detail so that someone else could read your description and grasp both what happened and why it was important.

   If you did not respond to the "simple test" in Chapter 1, do so now. But select only one moment or event and write a fleshed-out version of it in the manner just described.

2. Listed below are seven scenes or sets of "circumstances" taken from *Teaching with Your Mouth Shut*; you have been projected into each of them.

(a) You are a student in the class described in Chapter 1 in which the teacher does nothing but listen carefully to the students' discussion for the first two hours (pp. 8–9). The discussion is on *Hamlet*.

(b) You are participating in a discussion group with three other students working on the sequence of five questions called the Canary Problem in Chapter 6 (Appendix to Chapter 6).

(c) You are Emile and your tutor, Jean-Jacques, has pointed out the discrepancy between where the sun rises and where it sets and has then asked you, "How is that possible?" (p. 149).

(d) You are Emile and your carefully tended bean plot has been destroyed by Robert, the gardener (p. 150).

(e) You are a student in Ms. Green's open-ended seminar on Homer's *Iliad* described in Chapter 3.

(f) You are a student in a collegially taught class in which two teachers with very different points of view about the subject matter, psychology, invite you to join in the "conversation" about psychology they are carrying on in front of you and your classmates (Chapter 8).

(g) You are a student in the "political classroom" of Chapter 7 in which your teacher, Dr. Ford, refuses to "teach" you, insisting that "he will not tell you what to do." (pp. 111 ff.). In preparation for class, you have read *King Lear*.

You will be choosing two of these scenes to think about in more detail. To help you choose, take a moment or two and imagine yourself *in* each of the seven scenes, one at a time. For each, imagine what you would see and hear and what it would feel like to be a participant in that set of circumstances.

After you have gone through the list, select *two* that interest you. For each of these two scenes, write a brief "account" of your imagined experience participating in it. Let yourself go further than you did in your preliminary exploration above. Describe in writing what you see and hear, what you do, how it feels, and what happens as the scene develops. Write these accounts out in sufficient detail that another person could follow them. Write in the present tense using first-person pronouns (*I* and *we*).

3. You now have three texts before you, two describing scenes from the list above and one describing a scene from real life. [If you are in a group, exchange these documents so you have someone else's writing to read.] If you are working alone, try to alter your mental perspective

in what follows and imagine that these descriptions were written by someone else.

Your task is to consider what the three scenes have in common and how they differ. In order to answer these two questions, for each scene, ask yourself:

(a) Did significant *learning* take place or is it likely to take place? If so, what conditions were the critical ones? If not, why not? What obstacles got in the way or are likely to get in the way? What was absent that might have helped?

(b) Did good *teaching* take place, or is it likely to take place? If so, what were its critical features? If not, why not?

4. Based on your analyses above, what tentative conclusions (hypotheses to be tested in the future) about education can you draw? [To be done as a group, if you are in one.]

Part II: Concepts

1. The following is a list of concepts (central ideas) drawn from *Teaching with Your Mouth Shut.*

present interest	need	disequilibrium
environment	inquiry	immediate experience
reflection	Telling	"circumstances"
refusal	power	designed experience
problem-to-be-solved	authority	intelligence
thinking	intellectual experience	habit

Go back to the three written accounts you examined in Part I.

(a) For each, which concepts from the above list best help you make sense of it? (If you need to, locate and re-read the pertinent sections of *Teaching with Your Mouth Shut* to clarify any of the concepts.)

(b) Are there other concepts, not on the list and possibly not in the book, that you need in order to make sense of any of the three accounts you are examining? If so, what are they?

(c) Looking at the concepts you have designated for each of the three scenes in response to (a) and (b), are there any concepts that predominate? Which ones? Why do you suppose these concepts predominate?

2. One of the best ways to understand a conceptual point of view is to understand the links between the concepts that make it up. The fol-

lowing questions will help you do that for the conceptual point of view informing *Teaching with Your Mouth Shut*. Below are five pairs of concepts. They have been paired because they bear an important relationship to each other. For each pair, write a sentence or two explaining the connection or relationship between the two concepts. [If in a group, discuss the connection between each pair, and try to agree on the sentence or two that explains the connection.]

(a) Telling   (b) present interest   (c) intelligence
    inquiry   disequilibrium   reflection
(d) environment   (e) authority
    designed experience   refusal

3. Below are three phrases or sentences drawn from *Teaching with Your Mouth Shut*.

    1. ". . . beneath any product lies a process that made it." (p. 155)

    2. "Getting the teacher out of the middle" (pp. 103 ff.)

    3. ". . . no thought, no idea, can possibly be conveyed as an idea from one person to another." (p. 151)

    [If in a group, do the following as discussion questions and try to agree on answers.]

    (a) For each: If you had to explain to a friend interested in education but who hadn't read the book the meaning of the phrase or sentence, which two or three concepts from the list in question 1 would you rely on?

    (b) For each: Write a few sentences using the concepts you selected to explain the phrase or sentence to your friend.

Part III: Problems

Without consulting the book and in your own words, answer the following three questions in writing. [If in a group, discuss them and agree on an answer.]

1. How do parables "teach"?

2. In the *Meno*, Meno asks Socrates:

    How will you look for it [i.e., knowledge, the answer to a question], Socrates, when you do not know at all what it is? How will you aim to search for something you do not know at all? If you should meet with it, how will you know that this is the thing that you did not know?

    How would the author of *Teaching with Your Mouth Shut* answer Meno's question?

3. One of the quotations from Rousseau with which Chapter 9 begins reads: "All the instruments [of education] have been tried save one, the only one precisely that can succeed: well-regulated freedom."

   (a) What do you suppose Rousseau means by "well-regulated freedom"?

   (b) Make up an example of your own that illustrates "well-regulated freedom."

   (c) The phrase "well-regulated freedom" sounds like a self-contradiction. If the child is "regulated," how can he be "free"? Once freedom becomes regulated, does it not cease to be freedom? Make a case, in terms of your own example, that this phrase does *not* constitute a self-contradiction.

   (d) Now, write the best explanation you can of "well-regulated freedom."

Part IV: The Last Word

Answer questions 1 and 2 individually. If in a group, answer 3 also.

1. Review what you have written and thought during this workshop, and decide tentatively, for now, whether

   (a) you are convinced by the point of view of *Teaching with Your Mouth Shut,*

   (b) you are sympathetic with this point of view but think it needs revision or further development in some specific ways,

   or (c) you are neither convinced by this point of view nor in sympathy with it but find that an alternative point of view is needed to account for your experiences with learning and teaching.

2. If you decided (a), give your reasons. Discuss the particulars where contact between the book and your experience seemed the most compelling and persuasive.

   If you decided (b), discuss where the point of view of *Teaching with Your Mouth Shut* falls short and sketch out the needed revisions or development.

   If you decided (c), give your reasons and sketch out the alternative point of view that you think would better account for your experiences with learning and teaching.

3. [If in a group: (a) share your responses either by reading them or using them as notes to talk from, and then (b) discuss.]

Afterword

Ibegan my teaching career in 1967 while a graduate student in the Department of Social Relations at Harvard. I was one of the fortunate "teaching fellows" who, rather than acting as a teaching assistant for a professor, got to be a "house tutor" and teach a "group tutorial" in one of the residential Houses. Most of Harvard's departments require their majors to take a group tutorial as an introduction to the field during their sophomore year. Social Relations was an interdisciplinary department combining social psychology, sociology, and cultural anthropology. As a teaching fellow in the department, I designed and taught a yearlong weekly seminar on a broad topic in the field (e.g., "Interpretation in Social Science"). I taught this class for three years, shifting the topic each year.

I was left completely on my own to plan and teach this course. So I did what all new teachers do. I drew inspiration from the best teachers I had in college. The two teachers from whom I had learned most were in literature and philosophy, and they both ran their classes as seminars (in the Directed Studies program at Yale). We students would meet with our teacher around a table and he would pose us a series of focused questions about the day's reading assignment. We would struggle to answer the questions to the teacher's satisfaction, and he would gradually lead us to some conclusions about the meaning of the text. This is exactly what I did with my social relations students when I first began to teach. I prepared my sequence of questions carefully, and succeeded pretty well at re-creating the kind of classes that had excited me so much five and six years earlier when I was an undergraduate.

In 1970, I finished my doctorate, and became an assistant professor in psychology at the University of Washington. There I taught small graduate courses, moderately small undergraduate courses, and large lecture courses. It was lecturing that preoccupied me, since I had never done it before. Speaking to three hundred students through a microphone tied around my neck four days a week was a new challenge.

I spent the first year mastering the art of traditional lecturing and the second year realizing what an ineffective form of teaching it was. I was something of a specialist in Piaget's theory of intellectual development, and one day it dawned on me that if I believed what I was teaching my students about the way intelligence functions, there were implications I ought to be drawing about how to teach. Talking to students, telling them what to think, was completely antithetical to Piaget's view of the mind as an active, experimenting agency. If I believed Piaget, then I had to change the way I was teaching.

I spent the next several years experimenting with innovative approaches to teaching large courses, participating in an experimental "residential program" for freshmen and sophomores that had a brief life at the University of Washington in the early '70s, and looking for a job at one of the new alternative experimental colleges that were springing up all over during that era.

When I landed a job at my first choice among these colleges, I was raring to go. The Evergreen State College, unlike most of the other experiments of the '60s and '70s, was an institution unto itself (rather than a smaller program or college contained within a traditional institution) and had gone all the way in "clearing the necessary space" for a different kind of education. Evergreen had no academic departments, no tenure, no academic rank, no merit pay, no publishing or research expectations, no requirements for students, no majors, and no grades. Teams of faculty taught one interdisciplinary "academic program" (rather than course) at a time to students who took only one program at a time. Most of these programs lasted an entire year.

Evergreen was (and still is) a college that places no limits on its faculty's ability to experiment in teaching. For the past twenty-one years I have gotten to try out whatever teaching idea or approach I have been capable of dreaming up. Year after year, I have taught in closely knit teaching teams with colleagues who have introduced me to their favorite authors and thinkers. I have joined these colleagues in weekly "faculty seminars" as part of my routine work schedule, and I have witnessed them teaching in their own distinctive, imaginative ways. Evergreen has provided the ideal environment for someone like me, a teacher fascinated with the art of teaching and determined to do the best he can at it. After twenty-one years teaching there, I continue to feel privileged to work in an environment that values good teaching and that encourages its teachers to push to the limits of their intelligence to find the best ways to teach their students.

I spent the year 1996–97 on Sabbatical. I decided to write a book for a general audience that would set forth the view of teaching I had developed over my nearly thirty years of teaching. I have spent my career experimenting with, discussing, reflecting on, and writing about pedagogy. The time had come to pull my ideas together into a coherent whole and to make them public. *Teaching with Your Mouth Shut* is the result.

Bibliographic Note

For readers who wish to further pursue ideas they have come across in *Teaching with Your Mouth Shut*, I list below citations for all the books I have referred to.

Major Thinkers

Arendt, Hannah. 1958. *The Human Condition.* Chicago: University of Chicago Press.

Dewey, John. 1916. *Democracy and Education.* New York: The Free Press.

Freire, Paulo. 1968. *Pedagogy of the Oppressed.* New York: Herder & Herder. (Readers interested in Freire would do better to start with
> Freire, Paulo. 1980. *Education for Critical Consciousness.* New York: Continuum; and
> Shor, Ira. 1980. *Critical Teaching and Everyday Life.* Chicago: University of Chicago Press.)

Freud, Sigmund. 1966. *Introductory Lectures on Psycho-analysis.* New York: Norton.

Illich, Ivan. 1970. *Deschooling Society.* New York, Harper & Row.

Piaget, Jean. 1966. *The Psychology of Intelligence.* Totowa, NJ: Littlefield, Adams. (Readers interested in Piaget would do better to start with
> Piaget, Jean. 1967. *Six Psychological Studies.* New York: Vintage; and
> Furth, Hans. 1970. *Piaget for Teachers.* Englewood Cliffs, NJ: Prentice-Hall.)

Plato. 1961. *Meno, Phaedrus, Republic,* In *The Collected Dialogues of Plato,* eds. Hamilton and Cairns. New York: Pantheon.

Rousseau, Jean-Jacques. 1979. *Emile, or On Education.* New York: Basic Books.

Other Books

Parables

The Gospel According to Luke (16:1–8a). 1985. In *Anchor Bible*. Garden City, NJ: Doubleday.

Buber, Martin. 1966. *The Way of Man*. Secaucus, NJ: Citadel.

Reps, Paul. 1957. *Zen Flesh, Zen Bones*. Garden City, NJ: Doubleday.

Lectures

Bligh, D. A. 1972. *What's the Use of Lectures?* Harmondsworth, England: Penguin.

Gardiner, Lion F. 1994. *Redesigning Higher Education: Producing Dramatic Gains in Student Learning*. Report No. 7. Washington, DC: Graduate School of Education and Human Development, George Washington University (An ASHE-ERIC Higher Education Report).

Education

Finkel, D. L. & W. R. Arney. 1995. *Educating for Freedom: The Paradox of Pedagogy*. New Brunswick, NJ: Rutgers University Press.

Neill, A. S. 1960. *Summerhill*. New York: Hart.

Slater, P. 1966. *Microcosm: Structural, Psychological and Religious Evolution in Groups*. New York: John Wiley & Sons.

Index